W9-BHF-663

MAY - - 2017

THE
i heart naptime
COOKBOOK

THE
i heart naptime
COOKBOOK

more than 100 easy & delicious
recipes to make in LESS THAN ONE HOUR

JAMIELYN NYE

Creator of IHeartNaptime.net

GRAND CENTRAL
Life & Style
NEW YORK • BOSTON

Copyright © 2016 by Jamielyn Nye

Cover design by Laura Palese
Cover photographs by Jamielyn Nye
Cover copyright © 2016 by Hachette Book Group, Inc.

Hachette Book Group supports the right to free expression and the value of copyright. The purpose of copyright is to encourage writers and artists to produce the creative works that enrich our culture.

The scanning, uploading, and distribution of this book without permission is a theft of the author's intellectual property. If you would like permission to use material from the book (other than for review purposes), please contact permissions@hbgusa.com. Thank you for your support of the author's rights.

Grand Central Life & Style
Hachette Book Group
1290 Avenue of the Americas / New York, NY 10104
grandcentrallifeandstyle.com
twitter.com/grandcentralpub

First Edition: September 2016

Grand Central Life & Style is an imprint of Grand Central Publishing.
The Grand Central Life & Style name and logo are trademarks of Hachette Book Group, Inc.

The publisher is not responsible for websites (or their content) that are not owned by the publisher.

The Hachette Speakers Bureau provides a wide range of authors for speaking events. To find out more, go to www.hachettespeakersbureau.com or call (866) 376-6591.

Family photographs on pages ii, ix, xiv, 9, 227, and 259 by Angela Gerber Photography LLC
All other photographs by Jamielyn Nye

Print book interior design by Laura Palese

Library of Congress Cataloging-in-Publication Data

Names: Nye, Jamielyn, author.
Title: The I heart naptime cookbook: more than 100 easy & delicious recipes to make in less than one hour / Jamielyn Nye.
Other titles: I love naptime cookbook
Description: First edition. | New York, NY: Grand Central Life & Style, [2016] | Includes index.
Identifiers: LCCN 2016009475| ISBN 978-1-4555-6293-0 (hardcover) | ISBN 978-1-4555-6291-6 (ebook)
Subjects: LCSH: Quick and easy cooking. | LCGFT: Cookbooks.
Classification: LCC TX833.5 .N94 2016 | DDC 641.5/12—dc23 LC record available at https://lccn.loc.gov/2016009475

ISBNs: 978-1-4555-6293-0 (hardcover), 978-1-4555-6291-6 (ebook)

Printed in the United States of America

Q-MA

10 9 8 7 6 5 4 3 2 1

To my family & friends,
Thanks for loving
dessert as much as I do.
You are my favorite.

contents

♥

INTRODUCTION

Hi! I'm Jamielyn,
and I'm so glad you picked up this book.
Honored, really. If you love naptime and chocolate, I can
already tell we're going to be great friends!

I still can't believe it's official…I actually wrote a cookbook. This is the last thing I thought I would be doing five years ago, but it's funny where life takes you. You may be wondering what kind of degree I have in writing, or which culinary school I attended; but the truth is I never studied writing or cooking. I actually went to beauty school and worked as a hairdresser up until a few years ago. I've never really considered myself a great writer and definitely don't consider myself a professional cook. So how on earth did I come to write a cookbook and not only develop the recipes, but photograph every single one? *The answer has to do with that very special time of day: that blissful hour called naptime.*

· I Heart Naptime ·

AM I THE ONLY ONE who seems to crave chocolate once 1 p.m. rolls around and the kids are finally tucked in for their nap? I love my children more than anything, but there is just something about naptime that makes me want to sing, dance, and indulge in something sweet all at the same time.

When I first became a mom, everyone told me to nap when the baby naps. What they didn't tell me was that my free time would soon disappear and I would probably never pee alone again. For the first few weeks of my baby's life, I definitely took the advice to nap. After a month went by, I realized that if I kept napping, I would get absolutely nothing done that day. I was feeding, changing, or cuddling my sweet baby all day long. I enjoyed every single minute of it, but I quickly realized how precious naptime really was.

When my son was a baby, I learned that I had only about one solid hour to myself before naptime was over. I made sure to take full advantage of it. Most of the time I found myself in the kitchen. I'd throw dinner in the slow cooker, whip up something delicious for a little afternoon treat (hello, roasted bananas topped with Nutella and coconut), and then kick my feet up for a bit. That was *my* time, and it was heavenly.

I still remember a day back in October 2012 when my kids skipped their nap. In the short amount of time I took to go to the bathroom alone, my three-year-old son managed to dump my entire collection of sprinkles all over the kitchen floor, and my two-year-old daughter decided to paint the white kitchen island with bright red nail polish. This all happened in a matter of minutes. All I could do was laugh. Then cry. Then eat all the frozen cookie dough.

As I found myself cooking more and more during naptime, I began to fall in love with the art of food and what I was able to create at home in my own kitchen. I have always loved cooking. I remember helping my Gramma Ina in the kitchen whenever I went to visit. I would stir the big pot of potatoes for Sunday dinner. She would throw in a stick of butter and a pint of cream and tell me that's what made the potatoes delicious. It was my job to taste them to see if they needed a little more butter or salt, and I always snuck a few extra bites after tasting. I still, to this day, like to make that big pot of mashed potatoes (page 70) with plenty to spare for my family. I also remember baking all kinds of delicious goodies with my mom every Christmas and delivering plates to our neighbors. I still love carrying on that tradition.

My love for cooking seemed to grow stronger after I had a family of my own. I wanted to be able to create memories and introduce my children to recipes that have been passed down from generation to generation. There's also nothing better than hearing my kids tell me "That was the best ever!" after dinner or a special dessert.

I also learned that one of the best gifts you can give someone is something homemade with love from your kitchen. There's an undeniable satisfaction in taking someone a box filled with homemade treats and seeing how it can light up their day.

When I took a dish to someone's house, or to an event, friends and family would request the recipes. One declared my Soft Caramel Snickerdoodles (page 199) the *best* cookies they had ever had. Another said my Favorite Enchiladas (page 133) tasted better than the ones from their favorite Mexican restaurant. After my friends begged and begged for these recipes, I finally started writing them all down.

Then, one day back in October 2009, I decided it would be easier to keep my recipes stored online so I could send friends a link to the recipes they requested. At the time, I had absolutely no clue what a blog was and no idea where to begin. After a little research, I was up and running. I chose the name *I Heart Naptime*, with the intention of sharing all my naptime adventures. I posted all my favorite recipes, crafts, and whatever else I was working on at the time. Whenever someone asked how I made something, I would share it on the blog. For the first few months, I'm pretty sure that only my close friends and family visited the site, but I remembered one of my favorite quotes from the movie *Field of Dreams*: "If you build it, they will come." And that's exactly what happened.

My goal for the blog was and still is to inspire creativity. I love to motivate others to create new recipes and try a craft they've never considered before, or simply to brighten their day with my posts. I want to show other moms that they can still find time for themselves after having kids. I also want to help people realize you don't need to spend tons of time in the kitchen—and you certainly don't need to be a professional—to make something amazing for your family and friends to enjoy.

The blog that started as a naptime hobby soon became a full-time job for me. Before I knew it, I was supporting my family from the income made on my blog while my husband was in medical school and completing his residency. It wasn't easy trying to balance it all, but all that hard work has paid off. One of the rewards is this fun book—a collection of recipes that are simple, delicious, and can be prepped and prepared in under an hour.

· Why I Wrote This Book ·

AS I THOUGHT ABOUT WHAT I wanted this book to be about, I knew I didn't want it to be just another cookbook that sits unused on the shelf. I wanted it to be one you could use daily. I wanted to include classic recipes with a twist, recipes that have been passed down for generations, as well as fun new recipes I dreamed up, such as my Peanut Butter Brownie Ice Cream Sandwiches (page 207). Because, seriously…who doesn't love a good spin on brownies?

It was also important to me that all the recipes could be made (or thrown in the slow cooker) in under an hour. Let's face it…naptime isn't that long, and who has the time these days to spend hours in the kitchen? With hectic schedules and after-school activities, family dinner sometimes seems next to impossible.

I also knew that I wanted my book to include more than just recipes. Crafting is a big part of my blog and who I am, so I knew this book wouldn't be complete without a few quick-and-easy crafts. People always ask me how I have time for such "crafty" things, and I tell them you don't need to be Martha Stewart or have oodles of free time to create something beautiful. The reality is, we're all busy, and most days I'm just trying to keep my kids alive. I'm all about creating something beautiful with things I already have around the home. Quick, easy, inexpensive crafts are the best kind in my book! And *this* book is filled with them. If you're not the naturally crafty type, not to worry—I've included some helpful templates in the back of the book (and on my website at www.iheartnaptime.net/book-template) to make it easy for you to create these goodies and gifts at home.

It was so much fun putting together this cookbook for all of you, and I have to say it was quite a miracle I finished it on time. Just two days after I signed the contract for this book, I found out I was expecting. We were absolutely thrilled, as this was something we had hoped for! But then I panicked. The manuscript was due June 1 and my baby was due just one week later on June 8. How in the world was I going to cook, style, photograph, write, and edit this book, all while running a business with two young children, being pregnant, and having a husband who works more than eighty hours a week at the hospital? It didn't seem possible, but with lots of help from family and friends, prayers, and chocolate, I was able to get it all done two weeks early (and lucky I did, too, because my baby arrived early on June 1)! I will be forever grateful for the opportunity I had to write this book. I feel blessed beyond words to be able to do the things I love for a living.

I wanted to create a book that would be a reflection of the things I love to cook for my family and friends, and I feel very lucky I was given the opportunity to accomplish that.

I hope you'll enjoy this book as much as I loved making it for you. I hope you'll try new recipes and share them with a friend. Most importantly, I hope you'll find this book inspiring and helpful, and that it will be a book you open often.

What your children really want for dinner is YOU.

—DALLIN H. OAKS

· Getting the Whole Family Involved ·

MY KIDS HAVE BEEN IN the kitchen with me since the day they were born (thank goodness for slings)! Whenever I start cooking, no matter if it's dinner or dessert, my kids always come running in asking if they can help. No doubt, it is much faster and easier to cook alone, but I have created so many memories with my kids by letting them join in the fun. I think it's important for them to learn how to cook and develop a love for cooking, even at such a young age. It's also a great way to keep them entertained while I'm trying to make dinner. My kids still haven't realized that setting the table and doing dishes isn't "fun." I'm secretly hoping they never discover those are really chores!

Cooking together is an enjoyable activity for my family. An added bonus: I find that if I'm letting my children help with the cooking, they are more likely to eat what I make.

My kids love to help me make Fluffy Cloud Pancakes (page 22), homemade pizza (page 137), Fresh Strawberry Lemonade (page 177), Rainbow Cookies (page 195), and Sugar Cookie Fruit Pizza (page 203).

One of our family goals is to eat dinner together around the table at least four times a week. After the kids get home from school and my husband gets home from a twenty-four-hour shift at the hospital, I want us to be able to unplug from the rest of the world, sit down with one another, and just be together.

The rule at our house is that from 6 to 7 p.m., it's family time. All electronics are turned off, and for that hour we can just enjoy talking with one another. By setting aside one hour each day to spend as a family, we have built stronger relationships. While it doesn't always happen with our demanding schedules, we definitely try to make it a priority.

The kitchen is the center of our home, and it's a place I want everyone to feel welcome.

Each recipe in this book is meant to be not only approachable and easy to prepare, but a recipe your whole family will love. Each and every recipe was also tested (by myself and with the help of seventy-two recipe testers from all over the United States) to make sure they all came out perfectly. I will be forever grateful to all of my testers!

In the first chapter, I share my favorite things to keep on hand in the kitchen, my essential tips, and my favorite ways to stay organized by meal planning and cooking ahead with freezer meals. Then I share my favorite brunch recipes, lunch, dinner, party snacks, and dessert recipes. I also have some easy and practical crafty ideas sprinkled throughout the book, all of which can easily be made in under one hour. There is something in this book for every reader, every season, every mood, and every age-group.

Now, go have some fun, get messy in the kitchen, and share some yummy treats with the people around you!

a few of my favorite things

♥

Learn how to cook—
try new recipes, learn from your mistakes,
be fearless, and above all have fun!

—JULIA CHILD

Here I share some of my favorite ingredients and products to keep
in the kitchen. I could not live without these! I couldn't get through
a week without menu planning and freezer meals, so this book
wouldn't be complete without sections devoted to those time-saving
techniques. They've been a major help in keeping me organized, and
I hope you find them just as helpful as I do!

PANTRY STAPLES
--- & ---
KITCHEN FAVORITES

· Pantry Staples ·

HAVE YOU EVER STARTED TO make a recipe only to realize you're out of salt or baking soda? Me too! After running out of ingredients time after time and literally sending my kids over to the neighbor's house to borrow an ingredient, I finally decided it was time to get organized. Behold, my big giant list of pantry staples. Keep these ingredients on hand and write them on your grocery list the minute you run out, so you never have to go without fresh baked cookies again.

PANTRY

Chicken and beef broth/stock
Canned black beans
Canned kidney beans
Canned white beans
Canned diced tomatoes
Canned tomato sauce
Canned tomato paste
Long-grain rice
Dried pasta
Plain bread crumbs
Jarred salsa
Extra-virgin olive oil
Vegetable oil
Canola oil
Balsamic vinegar
Apple cider vinegar
Red wine vinegar
Lite soy sauce
Peanut butter
Jarred jam

BAKING

All-purpose flour
Granulated sugar
Powdered sugar
Brown sugar
Cocoa powder
Cornstarch
Old-fashioned oats
Baking soda
Baking powder
Active dry yeast
Sweetened condensed milk
Evaporated milk
Vanilla extract
Almond extract
Honey
Corn syrup
Chocolate chips (milk, semisweet, white)
Nuts (I love almonds, cashews, and pecans)
Marshmallows

SPICE CABINET

Kosher salt
Fine sea salt
Table salt
Black pepper
White pepper
Ground basil
Ground thyme
Dried oregano
Dried parsley flakes
Dried rosemary
Cajun seasoning
Ground cumin
Chili powder
Garlic salt
Garlic powder
Italian seasoning
Ground ginger
Ground cinnamon
Ground nutmeg
Cream of tartar
Ranch seasoning mix (such as Hidden Valley)
Taco seasoning

REFRIGERATOR

Milk
Eggs
Unsalted and salted butter
Cream cheese
Sour cream
Mayonnaise
Grated Parmesan cheese
Cheddar cheese
Mozzarella cheese
Greek yogurt
Yellow mustard
Dijon mustard
Ketchup
Barbecue sauce
Worcestershire sauce
Hot sauce
Bacon
Fresh herbs
Salad greens
Fresh seasonal fruit and vegetables

FREEZER

Chicken breasts
Ground beef and turkey
Frozen vegetables
Frozen fruit
Nondairy whipped topping

COUNTER

Bread
Yellow onions
Potatoes
Tomatoes
Garlic
Lemons
Limes

· My Ten Favorite Kitchen Tools ·

THESE ARE A FEW OF the kitchen tools I couldn't live without. They make cooking less frustrating and much more enjoyable!

1   **I ♥ MY STAND MIXER.** Not only does it look pretty on my counter, but it saves me so much time in the kitchen. I can't even count the number of times I've used it. I have two spare bowls and use them constantly.

2   **I ♥ MY SILICONE BAKING MAT.** This thing eliminates soaking and scraping cookie sheets and creates the perfect baked cookies. Put it on your Christmas list!

3   **I ♥ PRETTY MEASURING SPOONS.** I have at least a dozen sets and I love buying them in all kinds of fun colors. It's nice to have several sets on hand, so I don't have to spend time doing dishes in between baking different treats.

4   **I ♥ MASON JARS.** I use mason jars for all sorts of things—from storing pantry goods to making dressings and everything in between. Vintage ones are my favorite; I love to display them in my kitchen.

5   **I ♥ SHARP KNIVES.** Don't waste your time with cheap knives. Trust me, I've gone through quite a few sets from when we were first married and broke students. Once I invested in a nice set, I couldn't believe how much easier and quicker cooking became.

6   **I ♥ MY LE CREUSET CAST-IRON DUTCH OVEN.** It took me quite a few years to be convinced I needed such an expensive pot, but it was so worth it when I finally caved. You can find different brands of enameled cast-iron pots and also find them discounted at stores like HomeGoods. I love it because there's no need to season it. It goes from the stove to the oven at any temperature, cleanup is easy, and the colors are gorgeous! Plus, they last forever!

7   **I ♥ MY BLENDER.** I invested in a Blendtec high-speed blender a few years ago and haven't looked back. It makes the creamiest smoothies ever!

8   **I ♥ COOKIE SCOOPS.** I have them in small, medium, and large sizes, and use them all the time. The large ones are perfect for regular-size muffins and cupcakes. I use the medium ones for cookies; it saves me so much time when scooping out the dough. The small ones are great for making mini muffins.

9   **I ♥ MY SLOW COOKER.** It doesn't get any better than throwing together a meal in the morning and having it magically ready to go at dinnertime. If you don't have one, you need to get one for your birthday. Then try my Sunday Pot Roast (page 154). You'll thank me later.

10   **I ♥ MY FOOD PROCESSOR.** This thing can shred, chop, puree, and even make piecrust and scones (page 30). It's also great for making my Favorite Homemade Salsa (page 158)—it chops the onions and jalapeños so I don't have to!

SPICE JAR LABELS

PROJECT TIME 20 MIN

Spice jar label templates
(pages 252–53)

Cardstock paper

2-inch circle punch or scissors

Black fine-point permanent
marker

Mod Podge or glue

Foam brush

4- to 8-ounce jars

1 Photocopy the label templates on pages 252–53 or download and print from www.iheartnaptime.net/book-template. Cut out the labels with a circle punch or by hand. Handwrite the spice names you will be using onto the labels in permanent marker or use the premade labels.

2 Apply the Mod Podge to the back of the labels with a foam brush. (Alternatively, you can print the labels on label paper and simply adhere them to the jars.) Position the labels on the jars and press them on firmly. Allow to dry, then fill with spices.

3 Store in a cool, dark place.

MEAL PLANNING
··· 101 ···

What's for dinner? That's the question everyone
always asks when 5 p.m. rolls around. By this
time, if dinner isn't planned, I'll be the
first to admit that making a quick run through the
drive-thru or ordering pizza definitely crosses
my mind.

SINCE DINNER IS BOUND TO happen every night, why not make it easier on yourself? When I am on task and make my menu plan for the week, I save myself time, money, and stress. Not only do we eat out much less, but I also can avoid that daunting question: "What's for dinner, Mom?" I also try to let each of my kids pick a meal for the week, so I know they will like at least one meal I make.

Planning ahead is also the easiest way to ensure your family has dinner together each week. I love that saying "If you fail to plan, you plan to fail"—I find it so true when it comes to getting a nutritious meal on the table. I know I've had those weeks when nothing gets planned. Suddenly, it's Tuesday and I still haven't made it to the store, so I find myself picking up takeout for the second day in a row. Granted, I love to eat out more than anyone, which is why I've dedicated Saturdays to eating out. That is one day I don't cook, and we get to enjoy time out as a family. And sometimes my husband and I leave the kids at home and go out for a much-needed date night.

Menu planning really doesn't need to be complicated. If you set aside fifteen minutes each week, you'll save so much time and money in the long run. I promise!

· Getting Started ·

I RECOMMEND STARTING OUT WITH a five-day meal plan so you don't get overwhelmed. Then you can reserve those two extra days for leftovers or eating out.

Sit down with your calendar, favorite cookbooks, and computer, and start planning the week. Each week I usually try to rotate through our tried-and-true favorite recipes and also try at least one new recipe. You can ask your family for their favorite meals, so you can add a few of those to the menu each week.

Look through the lists of ingredients for the recipes you've picked and use those to create your shopping list. Most of the time I will look in my fridge and freezer to see if I can incorporate ingredients I already have on hand.

It's nice to try to plan meals that require fresh foods earlier in the week, so you don't need to make a second trip to the store. I like to plan a slow-cooker or freezer meal on days I know we'll be busy in the evenings. You can also try themed nights like Meatless Monday or Taco Tuesday to make it more fun. If your family tends to have a lot of leftovers, you can even dedicate one night to "cleaning out the refrigerator" so all those leftovers will get eaten up.

The next step is to make your big trip to the store. Planning your meals at the beginning of the week will keep you from having to make multiple trips to the store, and you'll waste less food. Make sure to bring your shopping list and check it twice.

When I plan my meals for the week, I try to use ingredients that I could use again for other meals, so I'm not throwing things out at the end of the week.

To save money, you can also plan your meals around what's on sale that week. I typically do my meal planning on Sunday evening and shop on Monday. It's amazing how much money you can save by shopping weekly sales and stocking up.

· Sample Meal Plan ·

HERE'S A SAMPLE MEAL PLAN you can use to get started. I've also included a simple menu board I created to keep me on task for the week. You can use a calendar or memo board to write down the meals for the week, too.

Menu

sun	Comfort Lasagna Soup (page 102) • Garlic Parmesan Asparagus (page 67) • Garlic Parmesan Breadsticks (page 53)
mon	BBQ Chopped Chicken Salad (page 91)
tues	Green Chile Shredded Beef (page 151)
wed	Stuffed Bell Peppers (page 126)
thurs	Leftovers
fri	Homemade Pizza Night (page 137) • garden salad • Homemade Buttermilk Ranch Dressing (see page 92)
sat	Eat out

DIY MENU BOARD

I created this menu board with chalkboard vinyl so I can easily write down what's on the menu for the week. It's simple to make and totally functional.
You could also cut out an 8 x 10-inch piece of scrapbook paper and place it in an 8 x 10-inch picture frame. You can use a dry erase marker to write on the glass and wipe it off each week. Easy peasy!

SUPPLIES

Sheet of chalkboard vinyl or
  chalkboard contact paper

Scissors

8 x 10-inch picture frame

Scotch tape

Chalk

Cut the chalkboard vinyl down to 8 x 10 inches. Remove the glass from the frame and replace the glass with the vinyl. I like to add a few pieces of tape to secure it. Place the back of the frame on to secure the vinyl in place. Then use the chalk to write down your menu. Use a wet cloth to wipe it down each week and plan the next week's menus.

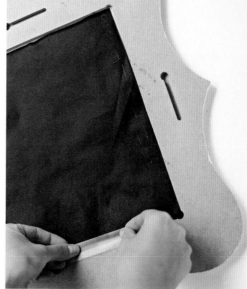

Menu

S: Pot roast
M: BBQ chicken salad
T: Taco soup
W: creamy pasta
R: stuffed peppers
F: Homemade pizza
S: Out to dinner!

FREEZER COOKING

Freezer cooking—cooking meals to freeze for later—saved me while I was writing this book. Some days, I literally cooked for ten hours straight. At the end of the day, I would freeze just about all of it. Then, on days when I was busy on the computer editing pictures or writing the book, I could pull out a homemade freezer meal for dinner and save myself from the guilt of picking up yet another pizza. When life gets busy and there's no time to make dinner, it's seriously nice to know there are premade meals in the freezer. I also stocked up big-time before I had my babies; let's face it, during those first few weeks, the last place I wanted to be was in the kitchen.

THERE REALLY ARE SO MANY possibilities when it comes to freezer cooking. One great way to get started with freezer cooking is to double a recipe when you're cooking dinner and then freeze half. Think about recipes your family already loves and start with those first.

Another great way to get started is to freeze individual ingredients. That way, you can add the ingredients to different recipes quickly. Some of my favorite things to freeze individually are precooked chicken (shredded, cubed, and grilled), browned meat, seasoned taco meat, sauces, fruits, vegetables, herbs, and so much more! Freezing is also a good option when you're left with half a can of an ingredient and aren't sure what to do with it.

I also love to flash-freeze foods such as bananas, berries, cookie dough, cookies, and other baked goods. To flash-freeze something, line a baking sheet with freezer paper or parchment paper and then place the slices or scoops onto the pan about one inch apart. Place the pan in the freezer for 30 minutes or until the food has firmed up. Finally, transfer the items to a freezer bag. The flash-freezing step ensures they won't stick together.

· Preparing Meals for the Freezer ·

FOR CASSEROLES AND THINGS THAT need to be reheated in the oven, place the food in an aluminum baking pan before freezing. These come in various sizes, and you can reuse them or toss them when you're done. I prefer the 9 × 9-inch size. I like to cover the top with aluminum foil and then place the whole package in a gallon-size zip-top bag for extra protection against freezer burn.

Transfer cooled soups, stews, and sauces to zip-top freezer bags and lay them flat in the freezer for easy storage. Make sure to squeeze as much air out as you can to avoid freezer burn.

You can also use reusable plastic or glass freezer containers, but I find that disposable containers make my life easier. They come in tons of different sizes and you can usually find them at the dollar store.

Once your food is packaged up, label the outside of the bag or foil with a permanent marker. Write down exactly what is inside and the date it was packaged. It may also be helpful to write down brief instructions for reheating, so you don't have to search for the recipe months later.

Avoid putting hot food in the freezer. Allow the food to cool on the counter or in the refrigerator before placing it in the freezer. This will help prevent freezer burn.

In addition, remember to clean out your freezer and rotate your stock meals every month, so you know what you have. Most frozen foods are best eaten within 2 to 3 months. Before I make my menu plan for the week, I like to look through my freezer and try to use freezer meals that need to be used up soon on an evening when the kids have after-school activities and cooking won't be possible.

FREEZER-FRIENDLY RECIPES

Here are some of my favorite recipes that freeze beautifully!

BREAKFAST

Fluffy Cloud Pancakes
(page 22)

Cinnamon Sugar French Toast
(page 26)

Perfect Crepes with Fresh
Raspberry Sauce (page 28)

Cheesy Ham and Spinach
Quiches (page 38)

Chocolate Chip Coconut
Banana Muffins (page 46)

Lemon Blueberry Yogurt
Muffins (page 42)

Apple Snickerdoodle Muffins
(page 45)

DINNER

Honey Butter Cornbread
Muffins (page 48)

One-Pot Taco Soup
(page 105)

Tomato Basil Parmesan Soup
(page 97)

Cheesy Broccoli Soup
(page 101)

Meat for Chicken Burrito Bowls
(page 147)

Creamy Chicken Cordon Bleu
Pasta (page 129)

Favorite Enchiladas
(page 133)

Chicken Hot Pie (page 110)

Cheesy Baked Ziti (page 122)

Baked Chicken Taquitos
(page 130)

Meat for Shredded Chicken
Tacos (page 140)

Meat for Sweet Pork Hawaiian
Haystacks (page 148)

Sunday Pot Roast (page 154)

Homemade pizza dough
(page 137)

BBQ chicken and cilantro
lime dressing (from the
BBQ Chopped Chicken
Salad with Cilantro Ranch
Dressing recipe, page 91)

SWEETS

Double Chocolate Chip
Sprinkle Cookies
(page 186)

Peanut Butter Brownie
Ice Cream Sandwiches
(page 207)

Sugar Cookie Bars with Cream
Cheese Frosting
(page 191)

Boyfriend Cookies (page 196)

White Chocolate Cranberry
Macadamia Nut Cookies
(page 204)

Caramel-Frosted Pumpkin
Cookies (page 210)

Banana Bars with Cream
Cheese Frosting
(page 237)

Chocolate Peanut Butter
Truffles (page 225)

Chocolate Mint Brownie Bites
(page 229)

rise & shine

♥

If you're afraid of butter, use cream.

—JULIA CHILD

My family loves to make a big Sunday breakfast, and pancakes, French toast, or crepes are usually on the menu. Some of my best memories are of my kids helping me stir the big bowl full of batter and flipping the pancakes, in our pajamas. These indulgent breakfast recipes are perfect for any day of the week, casual brunches, and even special occasions, and will be sure to make your family smile!

My kids also request breakfast for dinner almost daily, so we try to rotate one of these recipes into the dinner menu at least once a week. Pancakes and bacon for the win!

RECIPES

MAKES
ABOUT
6 CUPS

PREP
15 min

COOK
16–23 min

TOTAL
31–38 min

MAPLE ROASTED
granola

This homemade granola recipe is inspired by one my mom made growing up and is one of my favorite treats for breakfast. I've added a few different ingredients to spice it up, and it truly is the perfect granola. The brown sugar, coconut, and maple syrup blend together beautifully with the oats. I love to put this granola on top of yogurt with fresh berries. We also like to sprinkle it over ice cream with caramel sauce (page 242) for dessert.

Nonstick cooking spray

4 cups old-fashioned rolled oats

¾ cup sweetened coconut flakes

¼ cup packed light brown sugar

¼ cup chopped pecans

¼ cup sliced almonds

½ cup canola oil

⅓ cup honey

¼ cup pure maple syrup

1 teaspoon vanilla extract

1 teaspoon ground cinnamon

½ teaspoon table salt or fine sea salt

1 Preheat the oven to 325°F. Line a large rimmed baking sheet with aluminum foil and spray the foil with nonstick cooking spray.

2 In a large bowl, stir together the oats, coconut, brown sugar, pecans, and almonds. Add the oil, honey, maple syrup, vanilla, cinnamon, and salt and stir to combine.

3 Spread the oat mixture over the prepared pan with a rubber or offset spatula. Bake for 8 minutes, then remove from the oven and stir the granola. Bake for 8 to 10 minutes more, or until lightly golden brown. For extra-crunchy granola, cook for 3 to 5 minutes more. Remove from the oven, stir, and set aside to cool. It will be a little sticky, but it will harden as it cools.

4 After the granola has cooled, break it into pieces and serve with your favorite yogurt and fresh berries. Store in an airtight container at room temperature for 2 to 3 weeks.

HELPFUL · TIP ·

When measuring sticky or thick ingredients like honey, molasses, sour cream, or peanut butter, spray your measuring cup with nonstick cooking spray first. The ingredient will slide right out.

VARIATION Try adding dried fruit, wheat germ, or sunflower seeds to the mixture.

smoothie

SERVES
2–4

PREP
5 min

TOTAL
5 min

This berry smoothie is one of my family's go-to breakfasts. It's so easy to make, and your kids will never even realize they are drinking spinach. It's also packed with vitamins and antioxidants and is a natural energy booster. It's a great way to sneak in those fruits and veggies! Making this with frozen strawberries and blueberries is my favorite, but you can't go wrong with any berry combination.

♥

¾ cup 100% pure unsweetened apple juice

½ cup vanilla Greek yogurt (or use one 5-ounce prepackaged cup)

2 cups fresh spinach

2 small bananas

2 cups frozen mixed berries

1 cup frozen pineapple

1 Place the apple juice and vanilla yogurt in a blender. Add the spinach and bananas and blend until smooth. Add the frozen berries and pineapple and blend everything together. Add water as needed, up to ½ cup, to reach the desired consistency. Blend until smooth. Serve immediately.

smoothie

SERVES
2–4

PREP
5 min

TOTAL
5 min

Peanut butter and jelly sandwiches are made almost daily in my house. This smoothie has all the nostalgia of a classic PB&J made with peanut butter and homemade strawberry jam, but a lot healthier. This smoothie is extra creamy, sweet, and very filling.

♥

1 Place the milk and yogurt in a blender. Add the strawberries, raspberries, peanut butter, honey, and vanilla. Blend on high until smooth. Add more milk, if needed, to reach the desired consistency. You can also add another tablespoon of peanut butter for a nuttier flavor. Serve immediately.

1 cup low-fat milk, plus more as needed

1 cup vanilla Greek yogurt

2 cups frozen strawberries (about 12)

1 cup frozen raspberries or mixed berries

2 tablespoons creamy peanut butter, plus more as needed

2 tablespoons honey or agave syrup

1 teaspoon vanilla extract

MAKES
14
pancakes

PREP
15 min

COOK
10 min

TOTAL
25 min

pancakes

These pancakes are my kids' most-loved breakfast. They call them fluffy cloud pancakes because they are so soft and sweet. The nice thing about this recipe is that it's easy to double, so you can freeze half the pancakes for those mornings when you don't feel like cooking. They warm up nicely in the microwave or toaster in about thirty seconds. We love to serve them with Candy Syrup (page 29) and fresh strawberries or bananas.

♥

1½ cups low-fat milk, plus 1 to 2 tablespoons more, if needed

2 tablespoons distilled white vinegar

4 tablespoons (½ stick) unsalted butter, plus more for the griddle

2 cups all-purpose flour

¼ cup sugar

2 teaspoons baking powder

1½ teaspoons baking soda

¾ teaspoon salt

2 teaspoons vanilla extract

2 large eggs, whisked

Nonstick cooking spray (optional)

Candy Syrup (page 29), for serving

VARIATION This recipe makes great waffles, too. Instead of whisking the eggs whole, remove the egg yolks and beat the egg whites with a hand mixer until stiff, about 2 minutes. Then fold the whites into the milk mixture. Pour ½-cup portions of the batter into a hot greased waffle iron and cook until golden brown.

1 Preheat a griddle to 325°F, or heat a skillet over medium heat.

2 Combine the milk and vinegar in a medium bowl. Set aside for 5 minutes to sour. Put the butter in a small microwave-safe bowl and melt in the microwave. Set aside to cool for 3 minutes.

3 In a large bowl, whisk together the flour, sugar, baking powder, baking soda, and salt. Set aside.

4 Whisk the vanilla and melted butter into the soured milk. Whisk in the eggs and stir until well combined. Stir in the flour mixture with a wooden spoon, just until most of the lumps are gone and the batter is smooth. Add 1 to 2 tablespoons more milk if the batter is too thick.

5 Coat the griddle or skillet with butter (or nonstick cooking spray) and then pour ¼-cup portions of the batter onto the heated griddle. Cook 4 pancakes at a time, or as many as will fit comfortably. Cook the pancakes until bubbles appear on the top, about 2 minutes, then flip and cook on the other side for 1 minute, or just until lightly browned. Repeat until all the batter is gone.

6 Serve immediately, or place the finished pancakes on a baking sheet in the oven at 175°F to keep warm. Top with butter and candy syrup.

NOTE *Leftover batter can be stored in the refrigerator for 1 to 2 days. Cover the bowl with plastic wrap and stir before using.*

FREEZER
TIP

Let the pancakes cool
and then place them flat in a large
zip-top bag. Store in the freezer
for use within 2 to 3 months.
When ready to eat, reheat in the
microwave for 30 seconds,
or until warm.

SERVES
6
- - - - - -
PREP
15 min
- - - - - -
COOK
18–20 min
- - - - - -
TOTAL
33–35 min

CARAMELIZED

apple german pancakes

If there is one recipe that I remember most from my childhood, this would be it. Eating these German pancakes always reminds me of the days when my mom would make a double (or triple) batch of these pancakes. Nothing made my siblings and me happier than watching the edges rise up in the oven. I've dressed up my mom's classic recipe with cinnamon caramelized apples, which makes them truly divine.

1 **Make the pancakes:** Preheat the oven to 400°F.

2 In a large bowl, whisk together the flour, granulated sugar, and salt. Add the milk and vanilla and stir to combine.

3 Beat in the eggs one by one with a hand mixer. Take the time to beat each egg until creamy yellow, at least 10 seconds each.

4 Place the butter in a 9 × 13-inch casserole dish and put the dish in the oven for 2 to 3 minutes, or until the butter has melted. Remove the dish and pour the egg mixture immediately on top of the hot butter. Bake for 18 to 20 minutes, or until the edges are light brown and fluffy.

5 **Make the caramelized apples:** While the pancakes are cooking, in a large skillet, melt the butter over medium heat. In a medium bowl, combine the brown sugar, granulated sugar, and cinnamon. Stir in the apple slices, then add the apples to the skillet with the melted butter. Reduce the heat to low and cook for about 5 minutes, or until the apples are fork-tender and the sugar has caramelized.

6 Cut the German pancake into 6 large squares and serve immediately, as it tends to deflate over time. Top with the caramelized apples.

VARIATIONS You can also try these without the caramelized apples. Some other toppings include raspberry jam, fresh berries, lemon juice and powdered sugar, maple syrup, or cinnamon sugar.

For the pancakes

1 cup all-purpose flour

2 tablespoons granulated sugar

½ teaspoon table salt or fine sea salt

½ cup 2% milk

1 teaspoon vanilla extract

6 large eggs

3 tablespoons unsalted butter

For the caramelized apples

3 tablespoons unsalted butter

1½ tablespoons light brown sugar

1 tablespoon granulated sugar

½ teaspoon ground cinnamon

1 large Granny Smith apple, peeled, cored, and thinly sliced

HELPFUL · TIP ·

To soften brown sugar, place a piece of bread in the container for a day or two. You can also do this with cookies and baked goods. The bread will dry up and get hard, while the cookies will stay soft for days! This is another trick I learned from my mom.

french toast

Tired of soggy French toast? Whip up a batch of this cinnamon French toast, and you'll get rave reviews from everyone who tries it. The cinnamon sugar adds a sweet touch to an all-time favorite classic breakfast dish. These taste amazing topped with Candy Syrup (page 29) and fresh berries or bananas.

SERVES 6

PREP 10 min

COOK 10 min

TOTAL 20 min

♥

¼ cup all-purpose flour

1¼ cups half-and-half

4 large eggs

3 tablespoons light brown sugar

1 tablespoon vanilla extract

2 teaspoons ground cinnamon

2 tablespoons unsalted butter or nonstick cooking spray

12 thick slices bread, such as Texas toast or French bread

Fresh berries, for serving

Maple syrup or Candy Syrup (page 29), for serving

1 Preheat a griddle to 350°F or heat a skillet over medium-high heat.

2 Put the flour in a medium bowl. Slowly whisk in the half-and-half, then whisk in the eggs one at a time. Stir in the brown sugar, vanilla, and cinnamon and whisk until the batter is smooth.

3 Melt the butter on the griddle or in the skillet. Dip the bread into the egg mixture, flip the bread to make sure it is evenly coated, and then place the bread on the griddle. Cook 4 at a time, or as many as will fit comfortably. Cook for 2 minutes on each side, or until lightly golden brown. Repeat with the remaining bread. Whisk the egg mixture as needed if the cinnamon starts to rise to the top.

4 Serve immediately, or place the French toast on a baking sheet in the oven at 175°F to keep warm. Top with fresh berries and maple syrup or candy syrup.

FREEZER TIP

Let the French toast cool and then place flat in a large zip-top bag. Store in the freezer for use within 2 to 3 months. When ready to eat, reheat in the microwave for 30 seconds, or until warm.

MAKES
14–16
crepes

- - - - - -

PREP
10 min

- - - - - -

COOK
15 min

- - - - - -

TOTAL
25 min

perfect crepes

with FRESH RASPBERRY SAUCE

This recipe can be used for any crepe creation. We love serving these sweet crepes for breakfast or dessert, but you can also make them savory by omitting the sugar and vanilla and filling them with eggs, meat, and veggies. These crepes taste amazing topped with a fresh raspberry sauce and a little powdered sugar. Some of our other favorite toppings include fresh fruit, pudding, peanut butter, Nutella, and whipped cream. The leftovers freeze beautifully.

For the raspberry sauce

2 cups fresh raspberries

¼ cup granulated sugar

1 tablespoon unsalted butter

1 to 2 tablespoons water or lemon
    juice

For the crepes

2 cups low-fat milk

4 large eggs

1 teaspoon vanilla extract

1½ tablespoons granulated sugar

½ teaspoon salt

1½ cups all-purpose flour

3 tablespoons unsalted butter,
    melted and slightly cooled

Nonstick cooking spray, for the pan

Mascarpone cheese, for serving
    (optional)

Powdered sugar, for serving

1 **Make the raspberry sauce:** In a small saucepan, combine the raspberries, granulated sugar, butter, and 1 tablespoon water. Cook over medium-low heat, stirring, until the sugar has dissolved and the mixture is combined. Simmer for 2 to 5 minutes more, or until the mixture has thickened a little. Remove from the heat and transfer to a jar. (You can pass the sauce through a fine-mesh strainer first to remove the seeds, but I like to keep them in.) Set aside to cool.

2 **Make the crepes:** In a blender, combine the milk, eggs, vanilla, granulated sugar, salt, flour, and melted butter. Blend until the batter is smooth, 15 to 20 seconds.

3 Spray an 8-inch skillet with nonstick cooking spray and heat the pan over medium heat. Lift the pan away from the stovetop and pour in ¼ cup of the batter. Quickly rotate the pan from side to side, until the batter forms an even circle. Cook for about 1 minute, or until the edges are beginning to turn golden, then flip. Cook for 1 minute more, or until lightly browned. Remove from the pan and stack on a plate until ready to serve, or place on a baking sheet in the oven at 175°F to keep warm.

4 Spread the raspberry sauce in the middle of each crepe and then roll or fold the crepe. Serve with mascarpone cheese on the side, if desired, and sprinkle powdered sugar over the top.

candy syrup

This syrup is thick, creamy, and sweet like caramel. My kids call it candy syrup, and it truly is just that. We love to serve it on top of pancakes, French toast, waffles, and even ice cream. Try to resist eating it by the spoonful!

MAKES
1½ CUPS

PREP
5 min

COOK
10 min

TOTAL
15 min

♥

1 In a large saucepan, combine the buttermilk, sugar, and butter and heat over medium heat, stirring occasionally. Bring the mixture to a low boil, making sure to watch it, as it will bubble up. Reduce the heat to medium-low and stir in the baking soda. Keep stirring for 3 to 5 minutes, or until the syrup turns a golden yellow color. Immediately remove from the heat and stir in the vanilla and salt. Serve warm.

2 Store in a jar in the fridge for up to 2 weeks. To reheat, place in the microwave and heat in 30-second increments until warm.

½ cup buttermilk

1 cup sugar

½ cup (1 stick) unsalted butter, cut into cubes

1 teaspoon baking soda

1½ teaspoons vanilla extract

Pinch of salt

HELPFUL · TIP ·

Keep a well-stocked kitchen so you aren't running to the store daily. Use my pantry list (page 3) to get started, and add items to your grocery list when you're close to running out of something.

MAKES
12
scones

- - - - - -

PREP
25 min

- - - - - -

COOK
13–15 min

- - - - - -

TOTAL
38–40 min

BAKERY-STYLE

raspberry cream scones

These sweet raspberry and cream scones taste like they came straight from the bakery. They're tender and soft in the middle like a biscuit and slightly crispy around the edges—perfect for brunch or an afternoon snack.

♥

For the scones

1 cup fresh raspberries

¾ cup plus 1 tablespoon half-and-half, cold

1 teaspoon vanilla extract

1 large egg yolk, whisked

2 cups all-purpose flour, plus more for dusting

6 tablespoons granulated sugar

5 teaspoons baking powder

¾ teaspoon salt

½ cup (1 stick) unsalted butter, cut into ¼-inch pieces and kept cold

For the glaze

1 tablespoon unsalted butter

1 cup powdered sugar

1 to 2 tablespoons half-and-half

1 **Make the scones:** Preheat the oven to 400°F. Line a large baking sheet with parchment paper or a silicone baking mat.

2 Place the raspberries in the freezer until ready to use. You don't want them completely frozen, just slightly chilled.

3 In a small bowl, whisk together the half-and-half, vanilla, and egg yolk. Set aside.

4 In a large bowl or food processor, whisk or pulse together the flour, 5 tablespoons of the sugar, the baking powder, and the salt. Using a pastry cutter or the food processor, cut in or pulse the butter until the mixture resembles coarse crumbs. While stirring, slowly add the milk mixture and stir just until combined. Don't try to get the dough completely smooth; you want to avoid overworking it. Gently fold in the raspberries and refrigerate the dough for 5 to 10 minutes.

5 Dust the counter or baking mat with flour and then place the dough on the mat. The dough will be sticky, so lightly flour your hands and pat the dough into a 10-inch circle about 1 inch thick. Sprinkle the top with the remaining 1 tablespoon granulated sugar.

6 With a very sharp knife, cut the circle into 6 wedges, then cut those wedges in half so you have 12 triangles. Place them at least 1 inch apart on the prepared pan. Bake for 13 to 15 minutes, or until the edges are golden brown. Transfer to a wire rack to cool.

7 **Make the glaze:** Put the butter in a small microwave-safe bowl and melt in the microwave. Slowly stir in the powdered sugar and half-and-half. The glaze should be thick but pourable. Add another tablespoon of half-and-half if needed to reach the desired consistency. Drizzle the glaze over the top of the cooled scones.

8 These scones are best eaten the day they are made or the following day.

orange rolls

These orange rolls are super soft and have a delicious orange buttercream frosting. The fresh orange zest adds the perfect touch. These are a staple at our house for Christmas, Easter, and other holidays. They have a citrusy twist on your traditional cinnamon rolls. We all go crazy over them! Don't expect these to last long in your home.

MAKES
10
rolls

PREP
45 min

COOK
15–20 min

TOTAL
approx
60 min

♥

1 **Make the dough:** In the bowl of a stand mixer fitted with the dough hook, stir together the warm water, milk, butter, granulated sugar, egg yolk, and salt. Stir in the yeast and 1 cup of the flour. Add the remaining flour ¼ cup at a time, until the dough is no longer sticking to the bowl. Knead for 2 minutes. If the dough becomes too sticky, add a little more flour. (You can also make the dough by hand in a large bowl.)

2 Once the dough is nice and soft, cover the bowl with plastic wrap and set aside in a warm spot for at least 20 minutes.

3 **Make the filling:** In a small bowl, combine the butter, granulated sugar, orange extract, and orange zest and mix until smooth. Set aside.

4 **Assemble the rolls:** Preheat the oven to 350°F. Butter a 10-inch pie dish or a 9 × 13-inch casserole dish.

5 Punch down the dough and roll it out on a floured surface into a rectangle, about 10 × 13 inches. Spread the filling over the dough with a pastry brush. Beginning on one long side, roll up the dough and pinch the ends together. Cut the dough into 1½-inch pieces with floss or a large knife. Place the rolls cut side up in the prepared dish, spacing the rolls about 1 inch apart. Let the rolls rise for 5 to 10 minutes while the oven warms up. You can let them rise longer if you have the time.

For the dough

⅓ cup warm water

⅓ cup milk, warmed

4 tablespoons (½ stick) salted butter, melted, plus more for the pan

¼ cup granulated sugar

1 large egg yolk, beaten

⅛ teaspoon salt

1 tablespoon fast-acting yeast

1½ to 2 cups all-purpose flour, or as needed

For the filling

5 tablespoons plus 1 teaspoon salted butter, at room temperature

½ cup granulated sugar

½ teaspoon orange extract

Zest of 1 orange

For the frosting

4 tablespoons (½ stick) salted butter, at room temperature

1 to 1½ cups powdered sugar

Zest of 1 orange

1 teaspoon orange extract

1 to 2 tablespoons heavy cream or milk

recipe
CONTINUES

sweet orange rolls
CONTINUED

HELPFUL
· TIP ·

If it's a cool day, warm the oven to 200°F with a small pan of water set on the oven floor, then turn off the oven and set the dough in there to rise.

6 Bake for 15 to 20 minutes, or until golden brown. Remove from the oven.

7 **Make the frosting:** While the rolls are baking, put the butter in a large bowl. Slowly beat in the powdered sugar, orange zest, and orange extract. Add the heavy cream, 1 tablespoon at a time, until you reach the desired consistency. I like my frosting thick. Spread the frosting over the rolls while they're still warm.

A SWEET GIFT

Bake these rolls in an aluminum pan and, once they have cooled, wrap with plastic wrap. Then cut a piece of fabric (1½ inches thick) to tie around the top for a unique gift to give to a friend.

from the kitchen of:

Jamielyn

Have a very sweet day!

breakfast potatoes

These savory and delicious potatoes make a quick breakfast or weeknight side dish. They are simple to make and so flavorful! They pair perfectly with eggs and bacon. We also like to roll up these potatoes in a tortilla with scrambled eggs to make breakfast burritos. There are so many yummy ways to enjoy them!

SERVES
4–6

PREP
10 min

COOK
15–20 min

TOTAL
25–30 min

1 In a large skillet, melt the butter over medium heat. Add the onion and cook for 1 to 2 minutes. Add the potatoes and stir to combine. Reduce the heat to low and sprinkle the salt, parsley, and pepper on top. Make sure the potatoes line the pan in an even layer. Cook for 15 to 20 minutes, flipping the potatoes every 5 minutes. Don't flip them too often, as you want the butter to caramelize them. Patience is key.

2 Once the potatoes are browned and tender, turn off the heat. Taste and adjust the seasoning, then serve.

VARIATIONS Try adding 1 teaspoon minced garlic with the onions. You could also top the potatoes with bacon, cheese, chives, and sour cream to make a "loaded baked potato."

3 tablespoons salted butter

¾ cup chopped yellow onion

3 russet potatoes, unpeeled and cut into ½-inch cubes

1 teaspoon kosher salt, plus more to taste

1 teaspoon dried parsley flakes, or 1 tablespoon chopped fresh parsley

¼ teaspoon black pepper, plus more to taste

MAKES
12
mini
quiches

PREP
20 min

COOK
18—20 min

TOTAL
38—40 min

CHEESY

ham and spinach quiches

Quiche is one of our favorite breakfast foods to make for guests.
It's simple, filling, and always a crowd-pleaser. We love to use mini tart pans,
but muffin tins work great, too. These also freeze really well for when you
need a quick breakfast on the go.

2 (10-inch) refrigerated rolled
   piecrusts

1 tablespoon salted butter

¾ cup chopped yellow onion

1 boneless ham steak, cut into ¼-inch
   cubes (about ¾ cup)

¼ cup cooked bacon bits (optional)

5 large eggs

½ cup half-and-half

1 cup finely shredded sharp or mild
   cheddar cheese

½ cup finely shredded mozzarella or
   Parmesan cheese

½ teaspoon dried parsley flakes

¼ teaspoon black pepper

½ cup chopped stemmed spinach
   leaves

Once cooled, place the quiches
flat in a zip-top bag. Store in
the freezer for 2 to 3 months.
Reheat by cooking them in the
oven at 400°F for 5 to
10 minutes, or until warm.

1 Preheat the oven to 400°F.

2 Cut 4-inch circles from your unrolled piecrusts and
press the dough around the bottom and up the edges of
the mini tart pans or in the wells of a muffin tin. If using
tart pans, place them on a baking sheet. Pierce each round
of dough a few times with a fork. Bake for 5 minutes, then
remove from the oven and set aside. Keep the oven on.

3 Meanwhile, in a small skillet, melt the butter over
medium heat. Add the onion and cook for 2 minutes. Stir
in the ham and bacon bits (if using) and cook for 3 minutes
more, or until the onion has caramelized. Remove from the
heat and let cool.

4 In a large bowl, whisk together the eggs and half-
and-half. Stir in the cheeses, parsley flakes, pepper,
spinach, and the ham mixture. Pour about ¼ cup of the egg
mixture into each pie shell.

5 Bake for 18 to 20 minutes, or until the tops are golden
brown. Remove from the oven and let cool slightly. Serve
warm!

VARIATION Mix in your favorite veggies, such as asparagus, mushrooms, or tomato. This can also be made in a 10-inch pie pan with one
piecrust. Adjust the cooking time to 40 to 50 minutes.

pass the
butter, please!

♥

If baking is any labor at all,
it's a labor of love.

—REGINA BRETT

There's nothing more comforting than homemade
breads, rolls, muffins, and pastries. It just doesn't get better than
a warm muffin straight out of the oven with a big pat of butter
and a dollop of homemade jam.

Pull out your mixer and whip up one of these
scrumptious recipes.

---------------------------- RECIPES ----------------------------

MAKES
15
muffins

PREP
20 min

COOK
15–17 min

TOTAL
35–37 min

LEMON BLUEBERRY
yogurt muffins

Lemon blueberry muffins are made monthly at my house. The yogurt in these muffins makes them super soft and flavorful, but the sweet streusel topping takes them over the top. In a good way! I always freeze half the baked batch and pull them out when we need a quick breakfast or snack on the go.

-- ♥ --

For the batter

⅓ cup low-fat milk

⅓ cup vegetable oil

1 large egg

½ teaspoon vanilla extract

Zest of 1 large lemon

3 tablespoons fresh lemon juice

2 cups all-purpose flour

¾ cup sugar

4 teaspoons baking powder

½ teaspoon salt

¾ cup plain Greek yogurt or
    sour cream

1 cup fresh or frozen blueberries

For the topping

4 tablespoons (½ stick) unsalted
    butter, cold

5 tablespoons all-purpose flour

5 tablespoons sugar

Zest of 1 large lemon

1 **Make the batter:** Preheat the oven to 425°F. Line two muffin tins with paper liners.

2 In a large bowl, using a hand mixer, beat together the milk, vegetable oil, egg, vanilla, lemon zest, and lemon juice. In a separate bowl, whisk together the flour, sugar, baking powder, and salt. Slowly add the dry ingredients to the wet ingredients and mix until just combined. Avoid overmixing. Add the yogurt and stir until smooth. With a rubber spatula, gently fold in the blueberries, being careful not to break them.

3 Fill the muffin cups three-quarters full with the batter.

4 **Make the topping:** In a small bowl, combine the butter, flour, sugar, and lemon zest and cut in the butter with a fork or pastry cutter, until the butter bits are the size of peas. Sprinkle about 2 teaspoons of the topping on each muffin.

5 Bake for 7 minutes, then reduce the oven temperature to 375°F. Bake for 8 to 10 minutes more, or until a toothpick inserted into the center of a muffin comes out clean. Transfer the muffins to a wire rack to cool.

6 Store in an airtight container or zip-top bag. The muffins will stay fresh for up to 3 days.

FREEZER
❄
·TIP·

Place the muffins in a zip-top bag and press out as much air as you can. Store in the freezer for up to 3 months. When ready to eat, remove from the bag and warm in the microwave for 30 seconds.

APPLE

snickerdoodle muffins

These muffins are sure to make anyone's day just a little brighter. They have all the goodness of a snickerdoodle cookie baked into a muffin. The chunks of apples and cinnamon in every bite are a treat. Enjoy them at breakfast, as an afternoon snack, or as dessert.

MAKES
18
muffins

PREP
30 min

COOK
16–18 min

TOTAL
46–48 min

♥

1 **Make the batter:** In a medium bowl, stir together ¼ cup of the brown sugar, and 1 teaspoon of the cinnamon. Stir in the apple cubes and set aside.

2 In a large bowl, using a hand mixer, beat together the oil, granulated sugar, and the remaining ¾ cup brown sugar until combined. Add the eggs, sour cream, and vanilla and mix until smooth.

3 In a separate bowl, whisk together the flour, baking powder, nutmeg, the remaining 1 teaspoon cinnamon, and the salt. Slowly add the dry ingredients to the wet ingredients and mix until well combined. Fold in the cinnamon apples. Cover and refrigerate for 15 minutes.

4 Preheat the oven to 425°F. Line two muffin tins with paper liners or spray with nonstick cooking spray.

5 **Make the topping:** In a small bowl, using a fork, stir together the topping ingredients until the mixture is crumbly. Don't overmix. Set aside.

6 Using a large ice cream scoop or spoon, fill the muffin cups almost to the top. Sprinkle about 1 teaspoon of the topping over each muffin.

7 Bake for 5 minutes, then reduce the oven temperature to 375°F and bake for 11 to 13 minutes more. Insert a toothpick into the center of a muffin to make sure it comes out clean. Transfer to a wire rack to cool for 10 minutes.

8 **Make the glaze (optional):** In a small bowl, whisk together the powdered sugar and milk. Drizzle on top.

For the batter

1 cup packed light brown sugar

2 teaspoons ground cinnamon

1 large apple, peeled, cored, and cut into ¼-inch cubes

½ cup canola oil

½ cup granulated sugar

2 large eggs

1 cup sour cream

2 teaspoons vanilla extract

3 cups all-purpose flour

1 tablespoon baking powder

1 teaspoon ground nutmeg

¾ teaspoon salt

Nonstick cooking spray (optional)

For the topping

3 tablespoons unsalted butter, at room temperature

¼ cup granulated sugar

2 tablespoons all-purpose flour

2 teaspoons ground cinnamon

For the glaze (optional)

½ cup powdered sugar

1 tablespoon milk

MAKES
24
muffins
- - - - - -
PREP
15 min
- - - - - -
COOK
18–20 min
- - - - - -
TOTAL
33–35 min

CHOCOLATE CHIP

coconut banana muffins

These muffins are a sweet pick-me-up anytime of day. They have a nice banana flavor and are studded with chocolate chips and coconut flakes. Usually I will make half the batch with coconut and half without, since my kids prefer them plain, but I love them with the coconut. The baked muffins also freeze nicely, so you can pull them out for a snack on another day.

½ cup (1 stick) unsalted butter, at room temperature

1 cup granulated sugar

⅓ cup packed light brown sugar

2 large eggs

1 teaspoon vanilla extract

1 cup sour cream

2¼ cups all-purpose flour

2 teaspoons baking powder

1 teaspoon baking soda

1 teaspoon table salt or fine sea salt

1¼ cups ripe banana, mashed (about 3 medium bananas)

1 cup sweetened flaked coconut

1½ cups semisweet or milk chocolate chips

1 Preheat the oven to 375°F. Line two muffin tins with paper liners.

2 In a large bowl, using a hand mixer, cream together the butter, granulated sugar, and brown sugar. Add the eggs, vanilla, and sour cream and stir until just combined.

3 In a separate bowl, whisk together the flour, baking powder, baking soda, and salt. Slowly add the dry ingredients to the wet ingredients and stir until just combined. Fold in the banana, ¾ cup of the coconut, and 1 cup of the chocolate chips.

4 Using a large ice cream scoop or spoon, scoop the batter into the muffin cups. You want them about three-quarters full. Sprinkle the remaining ½ cup chocolate chips and ¼ cup coconut evenly on top of the muffins. Bake for 18 to 20 minutes, or until lightly browned and a toothpick inserted into the center of a muffin comes out clean. Transfer the muffins to a wire rack to cool.

5 Enjoy with a glass of cold milk!

NOTE *You can also divide the batter among four small greased loaf pans and bake for 35 to 45 minutes, or until a toothpick inserted into the center of a loaf comes out clean.*

DIY HALF APRON

PROJECT TIME: 20 MIN

Cloth napkin

Pins

Iron and ironing board

Scissors

1-inch ribbon (approximately 80 inches)

No-sew fabric glue or double-sided fusible tape

Lighter

1 First, determine how long you want your apron to be. Hold the napkin up to yourself or your child, fold the top part of the fabric down, and then place a pin there.

2 Warm up the iron and place the napkin right side down on the ironing board. Fold down the top edge to the pin (at least 1½ inches) and iron flat.

3 Cut your ribbon to 80 inches (more or less to fit) and then place the middle of the ribbon in the center of the flap. Using the fabric glue or fusible tape, line the fold and close the flap shut. Iron and allow to cool.

4 Tie the ribbon around the wearer and trim the ribbon down if needed. Use the lighter to seal the edges of the ribbon to prevent fraying.

MAKES
12–16
muffins

PREP
15 min

COOK
13–15 min

TOTAL
28–30 min

HONEY BUTTER

cornbread muffins

These tender and sweet cornbread muffins are super easy to whip up and are the perfect accompaniment for chili or One-Pot Taco Soup (page 105). The honey butter is a decadent treat to spread on top!

For the corn muffins

Nonstick cooking spray (optional)

¾ cup buttermilk, at room temperature

¼ cup honey

2 large eggs, at room temperature

1 cup yellow cornmeal

1 cup all-purpose flour

½ cup sugar

2 teaspoons baking powder

1 teaspoon table salt or fine sea salt

½ cup (1 stick) salted butter, melted and cooled slightly

1 (8.5-ounce) can cream-style corn

For the honey butter

½ cup (1 stick) salted butter, at room temperature

3 tablespoons honey

¼ teaspoon vanilla extract

HELPFUL
·TIP·

No buttermilk on hand? Add 1 tablespoon distilled vinegar or lemon juice to 1 cup milk and let it sit for 5 minutes to sour. That will do the trick.

1 **Make the corn muffins:** Preheat the oven to 400°F. Line a muffin tin with paper liners or spray with nonstick cooking spray.

2 In a small bowl, whisk together the buttermilk, honey, and eggs. Set aside.

3 In a large bowl, stir together the cornmeal, flour, sugar, baking powder, and salt. Add the milk mixture and stir just until combined. Stir in the melted butter and fold in the corn. (If you prefer not to have chunks of corn in the muffins, transfer the batter to a blender and blend just until smooth.)

4 Pour the batter into the muffin cups, filling them two-thirds full (you may need to use a second muffin tin). Bake for 13 to 15 minutes, or until golden brown and a toothpick inserted into the center comes out clean.

5 **Make the honey butter:** In a medium bowl, using a hand mixer, beat together the butter, honey, and vanilla until fluffy.

6 Serve the muffins with the honey butter. Store any leftover muffins in an airtight container or zip-top bag for up to 3 days. The honey butter will keep in the fridge for up to 1 month. Allow to come to room temperature before serving.

buttermilk biscuits

The most luscious, melt-in-your-mouth, buttery biscuits made in less than thirty minutes! Mix them by hand for the fluffiest biscuits. These taste perfect served plain, as well as with jam or honey butter (see page 48).

MAKES
10–12
biscuits

PREP
10–15 min

COOK
11–12 min

TOTAL
21–27 min

♥

1 Preheat the oven to 450°F. Line a baking sheet with a silicone baking mat or parchment paper.

2 In a large bowl or food processor, whisk or pulse together the flour, sugar, baking powder, and salt. Using a pastry cutter or food processor, cut in or pulse the cold butter cubes until the mixture resembles coarse crumbs. Slowly add the buttermilk and stir or pulse until just combined and the dough has come together. Add 1 to 2 tablespoons more buttermilk, if needed. The dough should not be too sticky and you should be able to roll it into a ball without it falling apart. Don't try to get the dough completely smooth; you want to avoid overworking the dough, so the biscuits don't bake flat.

3 Place the dough on a lightly floured surface and lightly pat the dough with your hands until it is about ½ inch thick. Fold each side of the dough over three times and then press it out to ½ to 1 inch thick.

4 Cut rounds of the dough with a 2- to 3-inch circle cutter or biscuit cutter and then place on the prepared baking sheet. Bake for 11 to 12 minutes, or until the tops are lightly browned and the biscuits are cooked through the center.

5 Brush melted butter over the tops when they come out of the oven and serve warm.

2 cups all-purpose flour, plus more for dusting

2 tablespoons sugar

1 tablespoon baking powder

½ teaspoon table salt or fine sea salt

½ cup (1 stick) salted butter, cut into ½-inch pieces and kept very cold

¾ cup buttermilk, plus more as needed

Melted salted butter, for serving

breadsticks

My family loves these breadsticks with Cheesy Baked Ziti (page 122) and Chicken Tortellini Soup (page 98). They are buttery, soft, and mildly seasoned, with great flavor. I like to make them when I'm in a hurry because they rise quickly. You can easily halve this recipe if you're cooking for a smaller crowd.

MAKES
16
breadsticks

PREP
35 min

COOK
12–15 min

TOTAL
47–50 min

♥

1 In a small bowl, mix together the warm water, yeast, and sugar until just combined. Cover with plastic wrap and let sit for 5 minutes, or until it begins to foam.

2 In a large bowl or in the bowl of a stand mixer fitted with the dough hook, combine 1½ cups of the flour and the salt. Stir in the yeast mixture and olive oil and begin to knead by hand or using the dough hook. Add the remaining flour, ½ cup at a time, and knead until the dough has formed a ball and is smooth, not sticky. Cover the bowl with plastic wrap and set aside in a warm place to rise for 15 minutes. It does not need to rise very high.

3 Preheat the oven to 400°F. Line two baking sheets with parchment paper or silicone baking mats.

4 Lightly flour the counter or a breadboard and divide the dough into 4 sections. Cut those 4 pieces into 4 smaller pieces. Lightly dust your hands with flour and roll each piece into a 6- to 8-inch breadstick. While holding the two ends, twist the dough until it becomes spiraled. As you form them, place the breadsticks on the baking sheets 2 inches apart, tucking the ends under.

5 In a small saucepan, melt 3 tablespoons of the butter over medium-low heat. Brush it over the breadsticks. Bake for 12 to 15 minutes, or until the bottoms of the breadsticks are lightly browned.

6 Meanwhile, melt the remaining 5 tablespoons butter. Stir in the garlic powder, Italian seasoning, parsley flakes, and Parmesan. Brush evenly over the breadsticks when they come out of the oven.

1½ cups warm water (about 110°F)

1 tablespoon active dry yeast

2 tablespoons sugar

3 to 3½ cups all-purpose flour, plus more as needed

1 teaspoon salt

1 tablespoon extra-virgin olive oil

8 tablespoons (1 stick) salted butter

¾ teaspoon garlic powder

½ teaspoon Italian seasoning

½ teaspoon dried parsley flakes

1½ tablespoons grated Parmesan cheese

MAKES
12
rolls

- - - - - -

PREP
40 min

- - - - - -

COOK
12–15 min

- - - - - -

TOTAL
52–55 min

one-hour rolls

This is one of my favorite roll recipes because they are quick and easy. The fast-acting dry yeast is a lifesaver when you're in a hurry because it cuts down the rising time by half, meaning you can have homemade rolls in no time! This recipe also doesn't make a ton of rolls, which is ideal for a small gathering. We love to eat these rolls with honey butter (see page 48) or homemade raspberry jam. If we're serving them with an Italian dish, I also like to sprinkle a little garlic salt and rosemary on top.

2½ to 3½ cups all-purpose flour, plus more for dusting

3½ tablespoons sugar

1½ teaspoons salt

½ cup low-fat milk

2 tablespoons fast-acting dry yeast

1 large egg, whisked

¼ cup vegetable oil

2 tablespoons salted butter, melted, plus more for the baking dish

1 In the bowl of a stand mixer or in a large bowl, whisk together 2 cups of the flour, the sugar, and the salt. In a small microwave-safe bowl, combine the milk and ½ cup water and microwave at full power for 45 seconds, or until it is lukewarm (about 110°F).

2 Mix the warmed milk and water into the flour mixture, then sprinkle the yeast over the top. Stir in the egg and vegetable oil until well combined.

3 Using the dough hook or your hands, add ¼ cup of the flour to the bowl and knead until the flour is incorporated. Add ¼ cup more flour if the dough still sticks to the sides of the bowl or isn't holding together. Add up to 1 cup more flour to achieve a dough that pulls away from the sides of the bowl and forms a ball. Knead the dough for 3 to 5 minutes. You want it to be nice and soft and not too sticky. (It's okay if it's still a little sticky.)

4 Preheat the oven to 400°F. Butter a 9 × 13-inch baking dish.

recipe
CONTINUES

speedy one-hour rolls
CONTINUED

5 Cover the dough with plastic wrap and place it on top of the oven. Allow the dough to rest for 15 to 20 minutes, or until it has risen slightly.

6 Turn out the dough onto a well-floured surface. Cut the dough into 4 equal pieces, then cut each piece into 3 equal pieces. Form each piece of dough into a ball and set them in the prepared baking dish. Set the dish on top of the oven for 10 minutes, or until they have puffed up a bit.

7 Brush the tops of the dough balls with the melted butter. Bake for 12 to 15 minutes, or until the tops are lightly golden brown. Transfer the rolls to a wire rack and brush the tops with more melted butter. Enjoy!

8 Store the leftovers in an airtight container or zip-top bag for up to 3 days.

baguettes

These French baguettes are a cross between a traditional crusty baguette and a soft French bread. They taste like heaven when you eat them fresh out of the oven. They're also great the next day for sub sandwiches, Garden Fresh Bruschetta (page 166), and making Homemade Italian Croutons (page 94).

MAKES
2
baguettes

PREP
30 min

COOK
15–18 min

TOTAL
45–48 min

♥

1 In a small bowl, combine the warm water, yeast, and honey. Cover with plastic wrap and let sit for 5 minutes, or until it begins to foam.

2 Put 1 cup of the flour in a large bowl or the bowl of a stand mixer. Stir in the yeast mixture and begin to knead by hand or using the dough hook. Add the salt and ½ cup of the remaining flour at a time until the dough is smooth but not sticky (you may not need all the flour).

3 Preheat the oven to 425°F. Line a baking sheet with a silicone baking mat or parchment paper.

4 Turn out the dough onto a floured surface and divide it in half. Gently roll one half into a 6 × 12-inch rectangle. Starting from one long side, roll the dough into a cylinder. Place the dough cylinder seam side down on the prepared baking sheet and tuck the ends under. Repeat with the second piece of dough. With a sharp knife, make three diagonal cuts across the top of each loaf. Let rest for 10 minutes.

5 Bake for 15 to 18 minutes, or until golden brown. Brush the tops with melted butter when they come out of the oven. Allow to cool slightly before slicing.

NOTE *For a crispier crust, brush the tops of the loaves with beaten egg white before baking.*

1¼ cups warm water (about 110°F)
1 tablespoon active dry yeast
1 tablespoon honey
2½ to 3 cups all-purpose flour
2 teaspoons table salt or fine sea salt
Melted salted butter, for serving

HELPFUL
·TIP·

When making yeast breads, make sure your yeast is fresh. Also, if it's a cool day, warm your oven to 200°F with a small pot of water inside; turn off the oven and place the dough in there to rise. You can also place the bowl with the dough on top of a heating pad to help the dough rise.

FRENCH BAGUETTE WRAP

There are lots of fun ways to package this baguette to give as a gift. It makes the perfect hostess or housewarming present. You can wrap the baguettes with parchment paper and twine to take to a friend, or wrap them with fabric and tie fresh rosemary or lavender to the top. And if you want to turn this into more of a gift, you can wrap the bread in a dishcloth and place it in a cute basket with a jar of jam, olive oil, or honey butter (see page 48) and bruschetta topping (see page 166). Now that's a treat!

SERVES
6—8

PREP
10 min

COOK
13—15 min

TOTAL
23—25 min

BALSAMIC

caprese garlic bread

This toasted garlic bread is topped with melted mozzarella, roasted tomatoes, and a balsamic reduction. I first tried caprese garlic bread at my favorite Italian restaurant and knew I had to re-create the recipe at home. It is so good and easy to make. This bread makes for one amazing side dish, appetizer, or even lunch! I could eat this every day and be happy.

---- ♥ ----

1 loaf French bread (sourdough or ciabatta also works)

½ cup (1 stick) salted butter, at room temperature

¼ cup grated Parmesan cheese

2 garlic cloves, minced (1 teaspoon)

1 teaspoon garlic powder

1 teaspoon dried parsley flakes, or 1 tablespoon chopped fresh parsley

Salt and black pepper

10 ounces fresh mozzarella cheese, cut into ¼-inch-thick slices

3 to 4 medium tomatoes, sliced

⅔ cup balsamic vinegar

3 teaspoons honey

¼ cup chopped fresh basil

HELPFUL
·TIP·

Buy minced garlic in a jar to save time. It makes things so much easier, and it will also keep your hands from smelling like garlic for the rest of the day.

1 Preheat the oven to 400°F. Line a baking sheet with aluminum foil.

2 Cut the loaf of bread in half horizontally and place it on the baking sheet cut sides up.

3 In a medium bowl, stir together the butter, Parmesan, minced garlic, garlic powder, parsley, and a pinch each of salt and pepper. Spread the mixture on top of the bread.

4 Next, arrange the mozzarella slices on top of the bread and top with the tomato slices. Season the tomatoes with salt and pepper. Bake for 13 to 15 minutes, or until the mozzarella has melted.

5 Meanwhile, in a small saucepan, bring the vinegar to a simmer over medium heat, then stir in the honey. Simmer for 3 to 4 minutes, or until the vinegar has reduced by about half and has the consistency of a thin syrup. Remove from the heat and place in a small bowl. It will thicken as it sits.

6 Remove the bread from the oven and let cool for a few minutes. Sprinkle the fresh basil over the top and drizzle with the balsamic reduction. Cut the bread into 2-inch slices and serve hot!

on the side

♥

Make each day your masterpiece.

—JOHN WOODEN

Turn up the heat and turn some of your ordinary
side dishes into something extraordinary! The fruit salad and pasta
salads are the perfect sides to bring to any potluck or as a
crowd-pleaser for family gatherings.

---------------------------- RECIPES ----------------------------

SERVES
4

- - - - - -

PREP
5 min

- - - - - -

COOK
25–30 min

- - - - - -

TOTAL
30–35 min

ROASTED

balsamic carrots

Growing up I absolutely despised cooked carrots. It wasn't until I was married and learned to roast them that I fell in love with the orange veggie. Roasting the carrots brings out the most amazing flavors—I could seriously eat the whole batch. They are absolutely wonderful and so simple to make. You can also swap the carrots for broccoli, bell peppers, or asparagus as a fun variation. I also like to make a big pan of mixed vegetables with this recipe.

♥

1 pound carrots, or 3 to 4 cups baby carrots

2 to 3 tablespoons extra-virgin olive oil, plus more as needed

1 tablespoon balsamic vinegar

2 to 3 garlic cloves, minced (1 heaping teaspoon)

1 teaspoon kosher salt, plus more to taste

¼ teaspoon black pepper, plus more to taste

Chopped fresh parsley (optional)

1 Preheat the oven to 400°F. Line a large baking sheet with aluminum foil.

2 Cut the carrots no larger than ½ inch thick and 4 inches long. (You can use baby carrots to make this step quicker.) Set the carrots on a paper towel to remove any excess moisture.

3 Place the oil, vinegar, garlic, salt, and pepper in a large zip-top bag. Shake until combined. Add the carrots and shake until the carrots are evenly coated with the mixture.

4 Spread the carrots in a single layer on the prepared pan. Bake for 25 to 30 minutes, tossing halfway through. The carrots will be lightly browned and fork-tender when done. Season with salt and pepper, and top with fresh parsley, if desired.

parmesan asparagus

This asparagus recipe is so quick and easy to make and goes well with just about any dish. I've even turned my "asparagus-hating" husband on to these. They are that good!

SERVES
4–6

PREP
5 min

COOK
9–11 min

TOTAL
14–16 min

♥

1 Cut off and discard 1 inch from the ends of the asparagus.

2 In a large skillet, melt the butter over medium-low heat. Add the garlic and cook for 1 minute. Place the asparagus in the pan and cook for 8 to 10 minutes, or until fork-tender. Flip the asparagus spears occasionally so they don't burn. Season with the salt and pepper.

3 Sprinkle with the Parmesan just before serving. Enjoy while hot.

1 bunch fresh asparagus, rinsed

2 tablespoons salted butter

3 to 4 garlic cloves, minced (1½ to 2 teaspoons)

½ teaspoon kosher salt

⅛ teaspoon black pepper

1 to 2 tablespoons grated Parmesan cheese

oven fries and fry sauce

Yup, homemade fries! During my last pregnancy, all I craved was French fries. I finally perfected the yummiest baked fries, so I could make a healthier version at home. These really are easy to make, crispy, salty, tender on the inside, and slightly addictive. For even more flavor, I like to sprinkle shredded mozzarella or Parmesan and parsley on top. They also taste amazing dipped in the fry sauce.

SERVES
4

PREP
10 min

COOK
30–35 min

TOTAL
40–45 min

For the fries
Nonstick cooking spray

3½ tablespoons canola oil

1 teaspoon kosher or fine sea salt, plus more to taste

¼ teaspoon black pepper, plus more to taste

¼ teaspoon garlic salt

4 russet potatoes, unpeeled, scrubbed and dried

For the fry sauce
¼ cup mayonnaise

2 tablespoons ketchup

½ teaspoon distilled white vinegar

⅛ teaspoon garlic salt

1 **Make the fries:** Preheat the oven to 450°F. Coat a large baking sheet with nonstick cooking spray.

2 Place the oil, kosher salt, pepper, and garlic salt in a large zip-top bag. Shake until the ingredients are mixed together.

3 Quarter the potatoes lengthwise and then cut the wedges into ¼-inch-thick French fries. Place the potatoes in the bag and shake until they are well covered with the oil and seasonings. Spread the potatoes in a single layer over the prepared pan. Bake for 20 minutes, then toss the fries with a spatula. Bake for 10 to 15 minutes more, or until golden and crisp.

4 **Make the fry sauce:** While the potatoes bake, in a small bowl, combine the mayonnaise, ketchup, vinegar, and garlic salt. Refrigerate for 15 minutes.

5 Remove the fries from the oven and season with more salt and pepper, if desired. Enjoy them while they're hot, dipped in the fry sauce!

HELPFUL · TIP ·

Clean as you go. My mom taught me this, and it helps me stay sane when I'm in the kitchen. It's also a great reminder of what already went into the dish. That way there's no wondering, "Did I already add the salt?"

SERVES
6–8
- - - - - -
PREP
15 min
- - - - - -
COOK
20–25 min
- - - - - -
TOTAL
35–40 min

CREAMIEST

mashed potatoes

Mashed potatoes are one of my favorite foods. I have been known to order mashed potatoes as a side wherever we go, just to find the best ones and see if I can improve on my recipe. I've tried making them so many different ways, but I have found that a few basic ingredients (including butter, of course… lots of it!) are all you really need to make the perfect mashed potatoes.

♥

- 2 teaspoons kosher salt, plus more to taste
- 3 pounds russet or Yukon Gold potatoes (about 8 medium), scrubbed and dried
- ½ cup (1 stick) salted butter, cut into cubes
- ¼ cup half-and-half
- ½ teaspoon black pepper, plus more to taste
- ⅓ cup sour cream

1 Fill a large pot with water and add 1 teaspoon of the salt. Bring to a boil.

2 Peel the potatoes, if desired, and quarter them. Place in the pot of boiling water and cook for 20 to 25 minutes, or just until tender. Drain the potatoes and return them to the pot. Gently mash the potatoes to release some of the steam. For extra-creamy mashed potatoes, pass the potatoes through a potato ricer.

3 In a small saucepan, melt the butter with the half-and-half over medium heat. Stir in the remaining 1 teaspoon salt and the pepper. Simmer for 1 minute and then remove from the heat.

4 Slowly add the butter mixture to the potatoes and mash to the desired consistency. If you want them extra creamy, use a hand mixer. Fold in the sour cream and season with salt and pepper.

5 Enjoy plain, with gravy (see page 154), or with melted cheese on top.

VARIATION Add 1 or 2 minced garlic cloves to the cream mixture for creamy garlic mashed potatoes.

i *heart* crafts

DIY NAPKINS

PROJECT TIME: 15 MIN

Fabric paint

Paper plate

Cotton swabs

6 cloth napkins (I prefer cotton)

1 Place the paint on the paper plate. Dab a cotton swab into the paint and then draw circles on the napkin. You can also create stripes, flowers, or other designs. If you have a stencil, you can add a monogram as well. Repeat with the remaining napkins. Allow to dry thoroughly before using.

2 Hand-wash only.

lime rice

Add a delicious flair to your rice by mixing in fresh lime and cilantro. This rice is one of our favorites to make with Chicken Burrito Bowls (page 147) and is the perfect side for any Mexican dish.

SERVES
4–6

PREP
10 min

COOK
20 min

TOTAL
30 min

♥

1 In a large saucepan, melt the butter over medium heat. Stir in the garlic and cook for 1 minute. Stir in the rice, broth, and lime zest. Bring to a boil, then reduce the heat to low. Stir the rice, cover the pan, and cook for 20 minutes, or until the liquid has been absorbed and the rice is tender.

2 Stir in the lime juice and cilantro, and season with salt and pepper to taste.

2 tablespoons salted butter

1 garlic clove, minced (½ teaspoon)

1 cup uncooked jasmine rice

1 (15-ounce) can chicken or vegetable broth (about 2 cups)

Zest and juice of 1 lime

3 to 4 tablespoons finely chopped fresh cilantro

Salt and black pepper

HELPFUL · TIP ·

Roll limes and lemons under the palm of your hand before juicing to ensure you get the most juice out of them. Also, use the tip of a spoon for easy juicing.

SERVES
6–8
- - - - - - - -
PREP
15 min
- - - - - - - -
COOK
10 min
- - - - - - - -
TOTAL
25 min

PESTO

caprese pasta salad

This pasta salad couldn't be any easier and is a great way to use up basil and tomatoes from the garden. My kids love picking the tomatoes for me, and we always sneak in a few tastes along the way. This salad is full of color and goes well with grilled meats tossed in or on the side. It is a crowd favorite and a great side dish to bring to a potluck or picnic. It is also totally suitable for a weeknight dinner.

♥

1 pound uncooked bow-tie pasta

1 tablespoon extra-virgin olive oil, plus more if needed

¾ cup basil pesto (or one 6-ounce jar prepared pesto)

¼ cup Italian dressing

1½ to 2 cups baby spinach, stemmed

1 pint cherry tomatoes (about 2 cups), sliced

1 (8-ounce) package bocconcini (cherry-size fresh mozzarella balls), drained and halved

Salt and black pepper

1 Bring a large pot of water to a boil and cook the pasta according to the package directions. Drain the pasta and run it under cold water to halt the cooking process. Transfer to a large serving bowl, drizzle with the olive oil, and stir. Let cool completely.

2 Stir in the pesto and Italian dressing. Add the spinach, tomatoes, and mozzarella. Toss to combine. Season with salt and pepper.

3 Cover the pasta and refrigerate until ready to serve. If the pasta seems dry before serving, you can stir in an additional 1½ teaspoons of olive oil.

NOTE *If making this salad the night before a party, add the spinach the next day. You may also leave out the spinach, if you prefer.*

VARIATION To turn this side dish into a meal, add 1 to 2 cups of grilled or shredded chicken and top with shredded Parmesan or feta cheese.

broccoli and bacon salad

This is a classic broccoli salad recipe that comes together
quickly and is always a crowd-pleaser. The thing that takes this salad over
the top is the bacon. It will make you want to actually eat broccoli
(and enjoy it), promise!

SERVES
8–10

PREP
20 min

CHILL
15 min

TOTAL
35 min

1 Combine the broccoli, bacon, nuts, grapes, and onion in a large bowl. Set aside.

2 In a small bowl, whisk together the mayonnaise, sugar, and vinegar. Pour the dressing evenly over the broccoli mixture and stir until coated. Season with salt and pepper.

3 Refrigerate the salad for at least 15 minutes before serving. This salad is best served the first day.

VARIATION Try grape tomatoes, dried cranberries, or strawberries instead of red grapes.

5 cups bite-size broccoli florets

5 bacon slices, cooked crisp, cooled, and crumbled

½ cup sliced almonds or cashews, or ¼ cup hulled sunflower seeds

½ cup red grapes, quartered

¼ cup finely chopped red onion

¾ cup mayonnaise or plain Greek yogurt

3 tablespoons sugar

2 to 2½ tablespoons white wine vinegar

Salt and black pepper

SERVES
6—8

PREP
15 min

COOK
10 min

CHILL
30 min

TOTAL
55 min

ZESTY

greek pasta salad

Pasta salad is one of my favorite side dishes to take to a potluck or get-together. It's simple to whip up right before the party and always the first to go. This salad is light, full of color, and refreshing, thanks to its tangy red-wine vinaigrette dressing. I am also known to make a big bowl of this pasta salad and eat it throughout the week for lunch.

♥

½ pound uncooked rotini pasta

¼ cup extra-virgin olive oil

3 tablespoons red wine vinegar

1 garlic clove, minced (½ teaspoon)

1 teaspoon Dijon mustard

½ teaspoon dried oregano

Salt and black pepper

1 pint grape or cherry tomatoes
   (about 1¼ cups), halved

1 cup diced cucumber

½ cup chopped red bell pepper

½ cup chopped red onion

½ cup sliced black olives (or one
   2-ounce can)

½ cup crumbled feta cheese

Chopped fresh parsley, for garnish
   (optional)

1 Bring a large pot of water to a boil and cook the pasta according to the package directions.

2 While the pasta is cooking, in a small bowl, whisk together the oil, vinegar, garlic, mustard, oregano, and salt and black pepper to taste. Set the dressing aside.

3 Drain the pasta and run it under cool water to stop the cooking. Transfer the pasta to a large bowl and add the tomatoes, cucumber, bell pepper, onion, olives, and feta.

4 Drizzle the dressing over the pasta and stir until evenly coated. Season with salt and pepper. Refrigerate for at least 30 minutes, or until ready to serve, to let the flavors marry. Serve garnished with fresh parsley, if desired.

CREAMY

hawaiian fruit salad

SERVES
8–10

PREP
15 min

CHILL
30 min

TOTAL
45 min

This fruit salad is so easy to assemble and perfect for a BBQ, holiday, or family gathering. One of our recipe testers claimed this was the best fruit salad she had ever tasted!

This recipe was inspired by the fruit salads my uncle Harold used to make for everyone who came by to visit. My uncle Harold had special needs, and he always loved to make people smile. I remember sitting at the counter when I was about eight years old, eating his famous fruit salad. We were both laughing about the fact that since I was born on leap year, I was *really* only two years old. Many good memories were made over this fruit salad! I think of Uncle Harold every time I make it.

♥

1 In a large bowl, using a hand mixer, beat together the cream cheese and sugar. Add the whipped topping and stir with a wooden spoon or spatula just until combined. Stir in the pineapple, grapes, apple, marshmallows, and coconut. Gently fold in the mandarin oranges.

2 Cover and refrigerate for at least 30 minutes before serving. The salad will keep in the refrigerator for up to 3 days.

1 (8-ounce) package cream cheese, at room temperature

1 tablespoon granulated sugar

1 cup frozen nondairy whipped topping, at room temperature

1 (20-ounce) can pineapple tidbits with juice, drained

1 cup halved red grapes

1 Granny Smith apple, cored and cut into ½-inch pieces

1 cup mini marshmallows

¾ cup sweetened coconut flakes

1 (15-ounce) can mandarin oranges in light syrup, drained

CHAPTER

5

soups & salads galore

♥

*People who love to eat
are always the best people.*

—JULIA CHILD

These soup and salad recipes make the perfect lunch or dinner.
I enjoy them for both, so I usually double the recipe to eat
all week long. I also love to freeze smaller portions of the soups, so
that I can pull one out for a quick and filling lunch.

------------------------------- RECIPES -------------------------------

SERVES
4–6

PREP
20 min

COOK
5–7 min

TOTAL
25–27 min

pomegranate salad
with CANDIED PECANS AND HONEY VINAIGRETTE

This is a simple-to-make and beautiful salad filled with lots of colors and textures. Hearty spinach, crisp pears, sweet pomegranate seeds, and candied pecans make a delicious and dreamy combination. The honey vinaigrette completes the dish and will have your guests begging for more. It is the perfect holiday salad thanks to its festive colors, but it can also transform any weeknight dinner into a celebration.

½ cup pecans

2 to 3 tablespoons sugar

¼ cup extra-virgin olive oil

¼ cup honey

3 tablespoons red wine vinegar

1 teaspoon Dijon mustard

1 garlic clove, minced (½ teaspoon)

½ teaspoon fine sea salt

¼ teaspoon black pepper

6 to 8 cups prewashed spinach or spring mix

1 large pear, peeled, cored, and thinly sliced

⅓ cup pomegranate seeds (arils)

3 to 4 tablespoons crumbled feta cheese

1 In a medium nonstick skillet, cook the pecans and sugar over medium-low heat, stirring continuously, for 5 to 7 minutes, until the sugar has melted and coated the pecans. Transfer to a plate and set aside to cool.

2 In a small bowl, whisk together the oil, honey, vinegar, mustard, garlic, salt, and pepper, or place the ingredients in a mason jar, cover with a lid, and shake until combined. Store in the refrigerator until ready to use and shake just before serving.

3 Place the spinach and pear slices in a large bowl. Sprinkle the candied pecans, pomegranate seeds, and feta cheese on top. Drizzle with the dressing and toss the salad until combined.

NOTE *For easier prep, buy prepackaged pomegranate seeds.*

VARIATION Apples and dried cranberries make great alternatives to the pears and pomegranate seeds.

mixed berry salad

with POPPY SEED DRESSING
AND CINNAMON ALMONDS

SERVES
6–8

PREP
20 min

COOK
5–7 min

TOTAL
25–27 min

This is a salad that makes me love spinach. Crave it, actually! I could eat it every day for lunch and be completely satisfied. But what really makes this salad extraordinary are the poppy seed dressing and the cinnamon-sugared almonds. You can even add grilled chicken to make it a more filling dinner salad. I often take this to a shower or a girls' lunch because it's sure to please.

♥

1 In a small skillet, combine the almonds, 2 tablespoons of the granulated sugar, and the brown sugar. Cook over medium heat, stirring, for 5 to 7 minutes, watching closely to keep it from burning. Once the sugar has melted and coated the nuts, sprinkle in the cinnamon and stir. The almonds may clump together. Transfer to a plate and set aside to cool. Break them into pieces once they have cooled.

2 In a blender or food processor, combine the oil, vinegar, salt, poppy seeds, and the remaining 4 tablespoons granulated sugar and blend until combined, about 30 seconds. Store in the refrigerator until ready to serve. Shake just before serving.

3 Layer the spinach and berries in a serving bowl and add the almonds on top. Drizzle with the desired amount of dressing, toss to combine, and serve immediately.

½ cup sliced almonds

6 tablespoons granulated sugar

2 tablespoons light brown sugar

1 teaspoon ground cinnamon

½ cup extra-virgin olive oil

¼ cup red wine vinegar

¼ teaspoon table salt or fine sea salt

½ teaspoon poppy seeds

8 cups fresh spinach

1 cup fresh strawberries, hulled and sliced

1 cup fresh blackberries

1 cup fresh raspberries

HELPFUL · TIP ·

Make the dressing and sugared almonds ahead and store in airtight containers at room temperature, so they are ready to go for quick lunches. They will stay fresh for the entire week.

ASIAN

chicken salad

One of my favorite local restaurants makes the most amazing oriental chicken salad, and I knew I needed to re-create it at home to share with you. This homemade version is so easy to make, not to mention much healthier than the restaurant version. You can modify this salad by adding whichever greens you have on hand.

4 to 6 cups romaine lettuce or spinach

1 to 2 cups classic coleslaw mix

2 cups cubed or shredded cooked chicken (I like to use rotisserie, chicken strips, or grilled chicken)

1 (11-ounce) can mandarin oranges, drained

¼ cup finely chopped green onions (optional)

½ cup sliced almonds or cashews

¾ cup wonton strips or chow mein noodles

⅓ cup mayonnaise

2 tablespoons rice wine vinegar

¼ cup honey

1 teaspoon Dijon mustard

⅛ teaspoon black pepper

Salt

1 Toss the lettuce and the coleslaw mix in a large bowl or four to six individual bowls. Place the shredded chicken, oranges, green onions, almonds, and wonton strips on top.

2 In a small bowl, whisk together the mayonnaise and vinegar. Whisk in the honey, mustard, and pepper. Taste for seasoning and add salt, if desired. Drizzle the dressing over the salad, using 1 to 2 tablespoons per serving.

3 Serve immediately.

BBQ CHOPPED

chicken salad

with CILANTRO RANCH DRESSING

This is such a simple and flavorful salad to throw together for a quick weeknight meal or get-together. It is so delicious and full of veggies, beans, and protein. It always gets rave reviews from anyone who tries it. This salad combines so many flavors I love in one beautiful dish, and the dressing is simply irresistible.

♥

1 In a blender, combine the buttermilk, mayonnaise, ranch seasoning, ¼ cup of the cilantro, the jalapeño, garlic, and lime juice. Blend until well combined. Refrigerate until ready to serve.

2 Layer the lettuce in a large bowl or four to six individual bowls.

3 In a small bowl, stir together the chicken and barbecue sauce until the chicken is well coated. Add to the lettuce. Layer the black beans, corn, tomatoes, remaining ½ cup cilantro, and the onion. Sprinkle tortilla strips on top, if desired; then drizzle with the dressing, using 1 tablespoon per serving. Season with salt and pepper.

VARIATIONS In the summertime, we like to use grilled BBQ chicken and grilled corn in this salad. On busy days, you can also place 4 or 5 chicken breasts and 1 cup barbecue sauce in a slow cooker and cook on High for 4 to 6 hours, then shred the chicken with a fork. Store the leftovers in an airtight container.

½ cup buttermilk

½ cup mayonnaise

1½ tablespoons ranch seasoning mix (such as Hidden Valley)

¾ cup chopped fresh cilantro

1 tablespoon minced jalapeño

1 garlic clove, minced (½ teaspoon)

Juice of 1 lime

8 to 10 cups spinach or romaine lettuce

2 cups shredded or cubed cooked chicken (I like to use a rotisserie chicken)

¼ cup barbecue sauce (I prefer a sweeter versus a smokier version)

¾ cup canned black beans, rinsed

¾ cup fresh or canned sweet corn

3 tomatoes, diced

¼ cup chopped yellow onion

Tortilla strips (optional)

Salt and black pepper

SERVES
4–6

PREP
15 min

CHILL
30 min

TOTAL
45 min

blt salad

with HOMEMADE BUTTERMILK RANCH DRESSING

This salad has all the goodness of a BLT, but it is much healthier. This will make a salad eater out of anyone. The homemade ranch dressing and croutons (page 94) make the salad, so don't skip them! Leftover dressing also makes a great veggie dip.

♥

1 cup mayonnaise

½ cup buttermilk, plus more if needed

2 tablespoons finely chopped fresh parsley

½ teaspoon garlic powder

¼ teaspoon onion powder

1 teaspoon distilled white vinegar or lemon juice

Salt and black pepper

6 to 8 cups chopped romaine lettuce (about 3 heads)

6 bacon slices, cooked crisp, cooled, and crumbled

1 pint grape tomatoes, halved

1 avocado, diced

1 cup Homemade Italian Croutons (page 94) or store-bought croutons

¼ cup shredded cheddar cheese (optional)

1 In a small bowl, whisk together the mayonnaise and buttermilk. Add the parsley, garlic powder, onion powder, and vinegar and stir until combined. Season with salt and pepper. Add an additional 1 to 2 tablespoons of buttermilk if needed to thin the dressing. Cover and refrigerate for 30 minutes before serving.

2 In a large bowl, layer the lettuce, bacon, tomatoes, avocado, croutons, and cheese (if using). Drizzle with the ranch dressing just before serving and toss to combine.

3 Any extra dressing will keep in an airtight container in the refrigerator for up to 7 days.

DIY UTENSIL HOLDER

PROJECT TIME: 10 MIN

Washi tape in the color of your choice

Widemouthed 32-ounce mason jar

1 Wrap the tape around the rim of the jar. Cut the tape and press it firmly against the jar. Add as many rows of tape as you'd like and then fill the jar with spoons.

2 Alternatively, you could apply the tape and then add colored acrylic or spray paint between the taped lines. Then remove the tape once the paint has dried for a striped design.

MAKES
4–5 CUPS

PREP
10 min

COOK
12–15 min

TOTAL
22–25 min

HOMEMADE

italian croutons

Homemade croutons take only minutes to make and are a great way to use up day-old bread. After trying these homemade croutons, you will likely never go back to buying store-bought ones. They have much better flavor and add just the right crunch to any salad (like the BLT Salad on page 92) or soup (like the Tomato Basil Parmesan Soup on page 97).

1 loaf day-old French bread or baguettes (page 57), cut into 1-inch cubes (4 to 5 cups)

2 tablespoons salted butter

2 to 3 tablespoons extra-virgin olive oil

1 teaspoon dried parsley flakes

½ teaspoon kosher salt

½ teaspoon dried basil

½ teaspoon garlic powder

⅛ teaspoon black pepper

1 Preheat the oven to 375°F. Line a large rimmed baking sheet with aluminum foil.

2 Place the bread cubes in a large zip-top bag.

3 In a small microwave-safe bowl, melt the butter in the microwave. Stir in the olive oil, parsley, salt, basil, garlic powder, and pepper. Let cool.

4 Pour the butter mixture into the bag and shake until the bread is evenly coated. Spread the bread cubes in a single layer on the baking sheet and bake for 5 minutes. Turn the croutons, then bake for 7 to 10 minutes more, or until the croutons are golden and crisp.

5 Enjoy on your favorite soups and salads. Store the croutons in a zip-top bag at room temperature for up to 2 weeks.

TOMATO BASIL

parmesan soup

As a little girl I loved classic tomato soup and grilled cheese. This recipe takes the traditional canned tomato soup to a whole new level. The fresh basil, oregano, and Parmesan add the perfect punch of flavor. And it tastes amazing when piled high with shredded cheese and Homemade Italian Croutons (page 94) or with a side of grilled cheese.

SERVES	6–8
PREP	15 min
COOK	30 min
TOTAL	45 min

1 In a large pot (I love to use my cast-iron pot), combine the oil and onion and cook over medium heat for 3 to 5 minutes, or until the onion becomes tender. Stir in the basil and oregano and cook for 1 minute. Add the tomatoes with their juice, chicken stock, and tomato soup. Bring to a boil, then reduce the heat to low and simmer.

2 Meanwhile, in a separate pan, melt the butter over low heat. Slowly whisk in the flour to make a roux. Cook for 2 to 3 minutes, or until the roux turns golden. Slowly whisk in the hot water until the roux is smooth and has thickened. Add the roux to the soup and stir well, then slowly stir in the half-and-half.

3 Once the mixture is well combined, stir in the Parmesan, salt, and pepper. Simmer over low heat for 20 minutes. Taste and add more salt and pepper, if desired. Serve with grilled cheese for the ultimate comfort meal.

1½ tablespoons extra-virgin olive oil

¾ cup diced yellow onion

2 tablespoons chopped fresh basil, or 2 teaspoons ground dried basil

1 tablespoon chopped fresh oregano, or 1 teaspoon ground dried oregano

2 (14.5-ounce) cans diced tomatoes, with juice

4 cups chicken stock

1 (10-ounce) can condensed tomato soup

5 tablespoons salted butter

⅓ cup all-purpose flour

1 cup hot water

1¾ cups half-and-half

1¼ cups grated Parmesan cheese

1 teaspoon kosher salt, plus more to taste

¼ teaspoon black pepper, plus more to taste

tortellini soup

This is a cheesy rendition on the traditional chicken noodle soup. We love this soup on a cold winter day served with Speedy One-Hour Rolls (page 54) or Fluffy Buttermilk Biscuits (page 51). The tortellini adds a delicious and filling twist, but this soup also tastes amazing with simple egg noodles.

SERVES
6

PREP
20 min

COOK
25 min

TOTAL
45 min

2 tablespoons salted butter

½ cup chopped yellow onion

2 garlic cloves, minced (1 teaspoon)

2 tablespoons all-purpose flour

4 cups chicken stock

4 large boneless, skinless chicken breasts, cut into bite-size pieces

4 large carrots, thinly sliced

3 celery stalks, thinly sliced

1 tablespoon fresh lemon juice

2 tablespoons finely chopped fresh parsley

½ teaspoon ground thyme

9 ounces cheese tortellini or egg noodles

Salt and black pepper

1 In a medium stockpot, melt the butter over medium heat. Add the onion and cook for 2 minutes. Stir in the garlic and cook until the onion becomes translucent. Slowly add the flour and stir until the mixture becomes a thick paste and turns a light golden brown.

2 Slowly whisk in the chicken stock and bring to a light simmer. Add the chicken, carrots, celery, lemon juice, parsley, and thyme. Simmer for 8 to 10 minutes, or until the vegetables are tender.

3 Stir in the tortellini and simmer for 8 to 10 minutes more, or until the tortellini and chicken are cooked. Remove from the heat and season with salt and pepper.

HELPFUL · TIP ·

Store spices in a cool, dark place (not above the stove) to keep their flavors longer. Also, make sure to restock your spice cabinet once a year to ensure your spices give out the best flavor. Spices will keep indefinitely, but they lose their flavor over time and are best used within 6 months to 1 year of opening.

broccoli soup

This broccoli and cheese soup is warm, rich, creamy…and ready to eat in thirty minutes! This is the ultimate comfort food when it's chilly out and incredibly fast to whip up. It tastes wonderful paired with warm rolls, garlic toast, or bread bowls.

SERVES
4–6

PREP
10 min

COOK
20 min

TOTAL
30 min

1 In a medium stockpot, melt the butter over medium-low heat. Add the onion and cook for 2 minutes. Stir in the garlic and cook for a minute more. Slowly whisk in the flour and cook for 1 to 2 minutes, or until the mixture is light golden brown.

2 While whisking, slowly add the chicken stock. Stir in the half-and-half and milk and simmer for about 5 minutes. Stir in the parsley, salt, and pepper. Stir in the broccoli and carrots and simmer, stirring occasionally, for 8 to 10 minutes. Cook until the broccoli is tender. If you like your soup more pureed, you can mash the broccoli with a potato masher or carefully transfer the soup to a blender and pulse. If you'd like to thin the soup, you can add up to ½ cup more milk.

3 Mix in the cheeses and stir until just combined. Season with salt and pepper.

4 Serve the soup hot. Stir just before serving.

- 4 tablespoons (½ stick) salted butter
- ¾ cup chopped yellow onion
- 2 garlic cloves, minced (1 teaspoon)
- ¼ cup all-purpose flour
- 2 cups chicken stock
- 1½ cups half-and-half
- 1½ cups 2% milk, plus more if needed
- ¾ teaspoon dried parsley flakes
- ½ teaspoon kosher salt, plus more to taste
- ¼ teaspoon white pepper or black pepper, plus more to taste
- 2 to 3 cups ½-inch broccoli pieces
- 1 cup French-cut (shredded) carrots
- 2 to 3 cups shredded sharp or mild cheddar cheese
- ⅓ cup grated Parmesan cheese

SERVES
4–6

PREP
20 min

COOK
21–23 min

TOTAL
41–43 min

COMFORT

lasagna soup

This soup has all the delicious flavors of homemade lasagna with half the work. It's one of those recipes everyone falls in love with. Every time I make this soup, my kids gobble it right up. We usually serve it with a big Italian salad and a warm French Baguette (page 57) or Garlic Parmesan Breadsticks (page 53).

♥

1 tablespoon extra-virgin olive oil

1 cup chopped yellow onion

3 garlic cloves, minced
    (1½ teaspoons)

1 pound Italian sausage, casing
    removed

4 cups chicken stock

1 (15-ounce) can petite diced
    tomatoes, with juice

1 (6-ounce) can tomato paste

1 teaspoon ground oregano

¼ teaspoon ground thyme

¼ cup fresh basil, chopped, plus
    more for garnish

8 uncooked lasagna noodles, broken
    into bite-size pieces

1 cup finely shredded mozzarella
    cheese

½ cup finely grated Parmesan
    cheese, plus more for garnish

Salt and black pepper

Ricotta cheese, for serving (optional)

1 In a large pot, heat the olive oil over medium heat. Add the onion and cook for 3 minutes. Stir in the garlic and cook for 1 minute. Add the sausage and cook, breaking it up with a wooden spoon as it browns, for about 10 minutes. Pour off any extra grease from the pan and slowly stir in the chicken stock.

2 Add the tomatoes with their juice, the tomato paste, oregano, thyme, and basil. Bring to a boil over medium-high heat. Add the lasagna noodles and cook until the noodles are tender, 8 to 10 minutes. Reduce the heat to low, then stir in the mozzarella and Parmesan. Season with salt and pepper.

3 Ladle the soup into bowls and top with Parmesan, fresh basil, and ricotta, if desired.

taco soup

SERVES
6–8

PREP
15 min

COOK
20–30 min

TOTAL
35–45 min

Taco soup is one of those dishes I make where I never follow a recipe. But I finally wrote this one down for you because it is by far the most requested meal at my house. My whole family loves it and my husband asks for it weekly. We first tried this at his Gram's house as newlyweds. It's a great meal for busy weeknights and freezes beautifully. We love to eat this soup with tortilla chips instead of spoons.

♥

1 In a large stockpot or Dutch oven, brown the ground beef over medium heat. Drain any extra grease from the pot. Stir in the onion and bell peppers and cook for about 3 minutes, or until the onion is tender.

2 Add the tomato sauce, salsa, diced tomatoes with their juice, black beans, kidney beans, corn, green chiles, cilantro, taco seasoning, ¼ cup water, and salt and black pepper to taste. Stir until combined. Cover the pot with a lid and simmer, stirring occasionally, for 20 to 30 minutes. This only gets better with time, so if you can, let it simmer longer. You can add up to ¼ cup more water if it starts getting too thick. Taste and add more taco seasoning, salt, or pepper as needed.

3 Ladle the soup into bowls and add your favorite toppings. Mine are fresh cilantro, sour cream, and shredded cheese.

1 pound lean ground beef

1 cup diced yellow onion

½ cup diced green bell pepper

½ cup diced red or yellow bell pepper

1 (15-ounce) can tomato sauce

¼ cup Favorite Homemade Salsa (page 158) or salsa of your choice (I like a chunkier salsa with traditional flavors)

2 (15-ounce) cans diced tomatoes, with juice

1 (15-ounce) can black beans, drained and rinsed

1 (15-ounce) can dark red kidney beans, drained and rinsed

1 (15-ounce) can corn, drained

1 (4.5-ounce) can green chiles

¼ cup chopped fresh cilantro (optional)

1 to 2 tablespoons taco seasoning, plus more to taste

Salt and black pepper

Optional toppings: chopped fresh cilantro, sour cream, shredded cheese, sliced avocado, and tortilla strips

FREEZER ·TIP·

Allow the soup to cool and then transfer it to a gallon-size zip-top bag. Seal the bag, pressing out any air, and then label the bag with the date and contents. Lay the bag flat in the freezer. When ready to eat, thaw in the fridge, then reheat on the stovetop over medium heat.

SERVES
6

PREP
10 min

COOK
20–40 min

TOTAL
30–60 min

LOADED

baked potato soup

This loaded baked potato soup is my go-to recipe when the temperatures begin to drop. It's super creamy and combines all the comforting flavors of a delicious baked potato in one amazing dinner. It's best served loaded with bacon, cheese, and chives—all the good stuff! It's worth the calories, promise!

♥

4 large russet potatoes, scrubbed

8 bacon slices

4 tablespoons (½ stick) unsalted butter

2 garlic cloves, minced (1 teaspoon)

¼ cup chopped yellow onion

⅓ cup all-purpose flour

2 cups low-fat milk

1 cup half-and-half

2 cups chicken stock

1 teaspoon kosher salt, plus more to taste

½ teaspoon garlic salt, plus more to taste

½ teaspoon black pepper

1 cup shredded mild cheddar cheese

1 cup shredded sharp cheddar cheese

1 cup sour cream

Minced fresh chives, for garnish

1 Pierce the potatoes multiple times with a fork, then microwave them for 12 to 15 minutes, or until tender. Alternatively, preheat the oven to 350°F and bake the potatoes for 45 minutes, or until fork-tender. Carefully halve the potatoes and let cool. Once cool enough to handle, remove the skins, and cut into chunks.

2 Meanwhile, cook the bacon in a skillet over medium-high heat until crisp. Transfer to a paper towel–lined plate to drain and cool. Reserve up to 1 tablespoon of the bacon fat from the pan, discarding the rest. Once the bacon has cooled, crumble it into small pieces.

3 In a large pot, melt the butter over medium-low heat. Add the reserved bacon fat, garlic, and onion and cook for 2 to 3 minutes, or until the onion is tender. Slowly whisk the flour into the pan and stir for 1 to 2 minutes. Slowly whisk in the milk and half-and-half. Keep whisking until smooth. Gradually add the chicken stock. Bring to a light simmer and whisk in kosher salt, garlic salt, and pepper. Keep at a light simmer until the mixture has thickened slightly, 5 to 7 minutes.

4 If you'd like to use cheeses and bacon as a garnish, reserve ¼ cup of each. Stir in the remaining cheeses, remaining bacon, and the sour cream. Remove the pot from the heat. Scoop potato chunks into the pan, breaking them into small pieces or leaving them chunky, depending on your preference. Serve hot, topped with your favorite garnishes, like cheese, bacon, and chives.

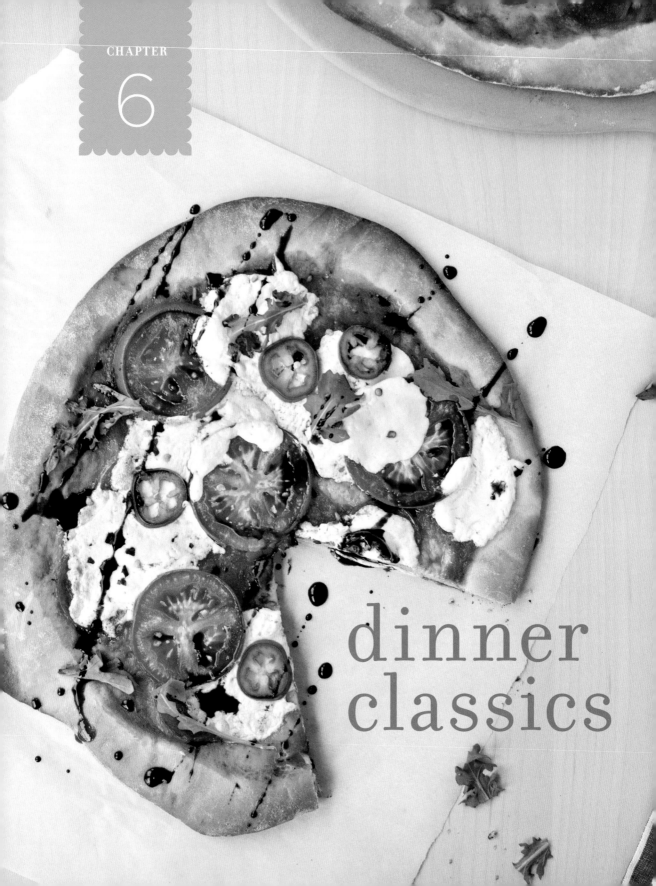

dinner
classics

♥

If you really want to make a friend,
go to someone's house...the people who give you
their food give you their heart.

—CESAR CHAVEZ

These are my family's go-to dinner recipes, the ones
that always seem to make their way into our weekly menus. I can
guarantee that they will please your whole family, picky kids
and all. And the best part? You can have dinner prepped and cooked
in less than one hour.

· · · · · · · · · · · · · · · · · · · RECIPES · · · · · · · · · · · · · · · · · · ·

chicken hot pie

SERVES
6

- - - - - -

PREP
30 min

- - - - - -

COOK
20–25 min

- - - - - -

TOTAL
50–55 min

Making homemade pies always make me feel domestic. I want you to feel domestic too! This recipe is fairly simple to make and a staple at our house, especially during the winter. We officially changed the name of this dish to "chicken hot pie" after my daughter repeatedly requested that we call it that. She always tells me that it's hot and not *in a pot, so naturally, it just made sense. This recipe does involve a little bit of work, but I promise it is worth it!*

4 cups chicken stock

1 pound boneless, skinless chicken breasts, cubed (about 2 cups)

1 cup diced potatoes (1 medium russet potato or 2 red potatoes)

1 cup sliced carrots

½ cup frozen green peas

½ cup sliced celery

2 (9-inch) unbaked piecrusts

4 tablespoons (½ stick) salted butter

¾ cup chopped yellow onion

¼ cup all-purpose flour

½ cup half-and-half

1 teaspoon kosher salt, plus more to taste

½ teaspoon black pepper, plus more to taste

⅛ teaspoon dried thyme, or ½ teaspoon fresh thyme, plus more to taste

HELPFUL TIP

For a lattice crust (shown opposite) use a pizza-cutter and cut even strips, about 1 inch wide. Then weave the strips across the top.

1 Preheat the oven to 425°F.

2 In a medium saucepan, bring the stock to a boil over high heat. Add the chicken, potatoes, carrots, peas, and celery and boil for 12 to 15 minutes, or until the chicken is cooked through and the vegetables are tender. Remove from the heat and reserve 1 cup of the stock for the filling. Drain the excess stock and set the chicken and vegetables aside.

3 While the vegetables are cooking, place one piecrust in a 9-inch pie pan and pierce the bottom with a fork a few times. Bake for 5 minutes.

4 In a large skillet, melt the butter over medium heat. Add the onion and cook for 2 to 3 minutes, or until soft and translucent. Slowly stir in the flour until smooth, and cook until lightly golden. Slowly whisk in the half-and-half and ½ cup of the reserved chicken stock. Stir in the salt, pepper, and thyme. Simmer over medium-low heat for a couple of minutes, or until it has thickened slightly. Remove the pan from the heat and add the chicken and vegetables. Add more of the reserved stock if the mixture is too thick. Taste for seasoning and add additional thyme, salt, and pepper, if needed.

5 Remove the piecrust from the oven and reduce the oven temperature to 400°F. Pour the chicken filling into the bottom crust. Cover with the top crust, seal the edges, and make five small slits in the top of the pie to allow steam to escape.

6 Bake the pie for 20 to 25 minutes, or until golden brown. Let cool for 5 to 10 minutes before serving.

chicken linguine

This linguine is tossed with chicken, asparagus, tomatoes, olive oil, lemon juice, and Parmesan cheese. You can also substitute the asparagus for broccoli. It's light on calories but big on flavor, and can be on the table in thirty minutes or less!

SERVES
4–6

PREP
10 min

COOK
20 min

TOTAL
30 min

♥

1 Bring a large pot of water to a boil and cook the linguine according to the package directions. Drain and set aside.

2 In a large skillet, melt 1 tablespoon of the butter with the olive oil over medium heat. Place the chicken, lemon pepper, and salt in a large zip-top bag. Shake until evenly coated and place the cubes in the pan. Spread the chicken out evenly and cook, stirring occasionally, until it is golden brown and cooked through to the center, about 8 minutes.

3 Transfer the chicken to a plate and set aside. Melt the remaining 1 tablespoon butter in the skillet and add the garlic. Stir in the asparagus, tomatoes, and parsley (if using). Cook for 5 to 7 minutes, or until the asparagus is tender. Return the chicken to the pan and add ½ cup of the Parmesan. Cook for 1 minute more.

4 Combine the noodles, chicken, and vegetables in the skillet. Add the lemon juice and the remaining ¼ cup Parmesan. Stir until combined. Taste and season with salt and black pepper.

½ pound linguine

2 tablespoons salted butter

1 tablespoon extra-virgin olive oil

1 pound boneless, skinless chicken breasts, cut into 1-inch cubes

1½ teaspoons lemon pepper

½ teaspoon kosher salt, plus more to taste

3 garlic cloves, minced (1½ teaspoons)

½ bunch asparagus (about ½ pound), cut into 2-inch pieces

1 pint grape tomatoes, halved

3 to 4 tablespoons chopped fresh parsley, optional

¾ cup finely grated Parmesan cheese

Juice of 1 lemon

Black pepper

SERVES
4

- - - - - -

PREP
20 min

- - - - - -

COOK
8–10 min

- - - - - -

TOTAL
28–30 min

JUICY

steakhouse hamburgers
with SPECIAL SAUCE

Grilling is one of my favorite things to do in the summertime. There's
nothing better than getting together with friends and family for a big ol' BBQ.
After you make these super-easy, super-delicious hamburgers, you'll never
go back to frozen patties again. And the special sauce takes these over the top.
They also pair brilliantly with Baked Oven Fries (page 68), Zesty Greek Pasta
Salad (page 78), or Pesto Caprese Pasta Salad (page 74).

♥

For the hamburgers

1½ pounds 80% lean ground beef

¼ cup shredded Monterey or Colby
Jack cheese

2 tablespoons barbecue sauce or
ketchup

1½ teaspoons seasoned salt (such as
Lawry's), plus more to taste

½ teaspoon onion powder

½ teaspoon black pepper, plus more
to taste

4 slices cheddar cheese (optional)

2 tablespoons unsalted butter, at
room temperature

4 hamburger buns

For the special sauce

¼ cup mayonnaise

1 to 2 tablespoons ketchup

½ to 1 tablespoon dill pickle relish

¼ teaspoon seasoned salt (such as
Lawry's), plus more to taste

Optional toppings: cooked bacon,
lettuce leaves, tomato slices,
sliced onion, pickles, jalapeño
rings

1 **Make the hamburgers:** Heat a grill to medium-high.

2 Combine the ground beef, shredded cheese, barbecue
sauce, seasoned salt, onion powder, and pepper in a
medium bowl. Mix with your hands until just combined.
Shape the mixture into 4 patties about ¾ inch thick. Indent
the center of the patties with your thumb to keep them from
bulging in the middle.

3 Grill the burgers for 4 to 5 minutes per side, or until the
center is no longer pink. If desired, top the patties with
cheese slices and grill until the cheese has melted. Remove
the burgers from the grill and set aside on a platter.

4 Spread the butter on the inside of the buns and place
them on the grill for 1 to 2 minutes, or until lightly
toasted.

5 **Make the special sauce:** In a small bowl, whisk together
the mayonnaise, ketchup, relish, and seasoned salt. Add
additional salt, if desired.

6 Serve the hamburgers on the toasted buns with the
special sauce and your favorite toppings.

QUICK AND EASY

chicken dinner

<table>
<tr><td>SERVES
4–6</td></tr>
<tr><td>PREP
10 min</td></tr>
<tr><td>COOK
35–40 min</td></tr>
<tr><td>TOTAL
45–50 min</td></tr>
</table>

One of the things I receive the most requests for on my blog is an *easy* dinner recipe. This is one of those dinners, and it is just right for a busy weeknight. It takes less than ten minutes to throw together and requires few ingredients. My kids always gobble this up, too, which is a huge plus—everyone can sit down at the table together and enjoy.

1 Preheat the oven to 400°F. Line a 9 × 13-inch baking pan with aluminum foil and place the chicken in the center of the pan. Place the vegetables around the outer edges of the pan. Drizzle the olive oil over the vegetables and chicken and sprinkle the ranch seasoning on top.

2 Cover the pan with foil and bake for 30 minutes. Remove the foil and sprinkle the Parmesan on top of the chicken and vegetables. Bake for 5 to 10 minutes more, or until the vegetables are tender.

3 Remove from the oven and stir the vegetables around. Season with salt and pepper and top with parsley, if desired.

VARIATION You can use Italian seasoning mix, your favorite herbs, and substitute different vegetables.

1 pound boneless, skinless chicken breasts

3 cups fresh broccoli florets or green beans

4 red potatoes, thinly sliced or quartered

¼ cup extra-virgin olive oil, or 4 tablespoons (½ stick) salted butter, melted

1 (1-ounce) package ranch seasoning mix (such as Hidden Valley)

2 to 3 tablespoons grated Parmesan cheese

Kosher salt and black pepper

Chopped fresh parsley, for serving (optional)

HELPFUL · TIP ·

Take away the stress of cooking daily by prepping ahead. At the beginning of each week I like to chop all my vegetables. That way I have everything ready to go.

SERVES
4—6

PREP
30 min

COOK
20—25 min

TOTAL
50—55 min

BAKED
sweet-and-sour chicken

After tasting this sweet-and-sour chicken, you'll never want to order Chinese takeout again. The chicken is fried, coated with a sweet-and-sour sauce, and then baked to perfection. The homemade sauce is what really makes this recipe. Trust me, it's worth a little extra work in the kitchen.

♥

For the chicken

Nonstick cooking spray

¾ cup cornstarch

¾ teaspoon kosher salt

¾ teaspoon black pepper

½ teaspoon garlic salt

1½ pounds boneless, skinless chicken breasts, cut into 2-inch cubes

3 large eggs, beaten

1 cup canola oil

For the sweet-and-sour sauce

1 cup sugar

⅔ cup rice vinegar or distilled white vinegar

⅓ cup ketchup

1 tablespoon cornstarch

1 tablespoon soy sauce

½ teaspoon garlic salt

½ teaspoon black pepper, plus more to taste

3 cups cooked white or brown rice, for serving

Steamed vegetables, for serving

1 **Make the chicken:** Preheat the oven to 375°F. Line a large rimmed baking sheet with aluminum foil. Coat the foil with nonstick cooking spray.

2 Place the cornstarch, kosher salt, pepper, and garlic salt in a large zip-top bag and shake until combined. Add the chicken and shake until the pieces are evenly coated. Beat the eggs in a bowl and have them nearby.

3 In a large skillet, heat the oil over medium heat until a drop of water sizzles when it hits the surface. Dip the chicken pieces into the beaten egg, then carefully transfer to the skillet with a fork. Fry the chicken for about 1 minute on each side, or until lightly browned.

4 Transfer the chicken to the prepared baking sheet.

5 **Make the sweet-and-sour sauce:** In a medium saucepan, whisk together the sugar, vinegar, ketchup, cornstarch, soy sauce, garlic salt, and pepper. Cook over medium heat, stirring, for 3 to 5 minutes, or until the sauce has begun to thicken. Taste and add more black pepper, if needed. Remove from the heat and set aside ¼ cup of the sauce for serving.

6 Pour the remaining sauce evenly over the chicken and bake for 20 to 25 minutes, or until the chicken is crispy and caramelized. Stir the chicken halfway through to ensure it doesn't stick to the pan.

7 Serve the chicken on top of the rice with the reserved sauce drizzled on top, along with a side of your favorite steamed veggies.

HELPFUL TIP

Take the time to read through the entire recipe before you start cooking. If I'm following a recipe, I always read through it first and pull out all the ingredients to make sure I have everything on hand. This procedure will prevent a dish from burning while you're searching for the next ingredient and ensure no ingredient is left out.

shish kebabs

These shish kebabs are perfect for a weeknight meal or a summer gathering with family and friends. Try different fruits and vegetables such as pineapple, peaches, tomatoes, and onions for a fun twist. The marinade is full of all kinds of delicious flavors and tastes great with steak or chicken.

SERVES
6

PREP
5 min

REST
30 min

COOK
10–15 min

TOTAL
45–50 min

1 In a small bowl, whisk together the oil, soy sauce, vinegar, lemon juice, brown sugar, garlic, salt, and pepper. Taste and add more salt and pepper, if needed. Reserve ¼ cup of the marinade for basting. Place the meat of your choice in a large zip-top bag and then drizzle the marinade over the meat. Shake until combined. Marinate in the refrigerator for at least 30 minutes. If you have more time, let it marinate longer.

2 If using wooden skewers, soak in warm water for 15 minutes to prevent them from burning. Heat a grill to medium-high. Thread the meat and vegetables onto the skewers. Place the skewers on the grill and brush with the reserved marinade. Turn the skewers until nicely browned on all sides and the meat is no longer pink, 10 to 15 minutes. Season with salt and black pepper before serving, if desired.

VARIATION We also love to marinate whole chicken breasts or steaks for a quick weeknight meal.

Heat a grill to medium-high. Place the meat on the grill and close the lid. Flip the meat after 6 to 8 minutes and brush with the reserved marinade. Cook the other side for 4 to 5 minutes, or until the meat is no longer pink. Season with salt and pepper before serving, if desired.

For the marinade

½ cup extra-virgin olive oil

¼ cup light soy sauce

¼ cup apple cider vinegar

Juice of 1 lemon

⅓ cup packed light brown sugar

4 garlic cloves, minced (2 teaspoons)

2 teaspoons kosher salt, plus more to taste

½ teaspoon black pepper, plus more to taste

2 to 3 pounds boneless, skinless chicken breasts or sirloin steaks, cut into 2-inch pieces

For the shish kebabs

12 cherry tomatoes

2 zucchini, sliced crosswise into rounds

1 orange bell pepper, chopped into 2-inch pieces

1 red bell pepper, chopped into 2-inch pieces

1 yellow bell pepper, chopped into 2-inch pieces

Salt and black pepper

SERVES
8–10

- - - - - -

PREP
20 min

- - - - - -

COOK
20–25 min

- - - - - -

TOTAL
40–45 min

CHEESY

baked ziti

This is my go-to meal when I'm having company over or taking a meal to a friend. It makes enough for two small families, and even the pickiest eaters will love it. This pasta is made at least once a month at my house! This dish tastes wonderful served with Balsamic Caprese Garlic Bread (page 60) or Garlic Parmesan Breadsticks (page 53) and a side salad.

♥

Nonstick cooking spray

1 pound ziti or penne

1 tablespoon extra-virgin olive oil

1 cup chopped yellow onion

4 garlic cloves, minced (2 teaspoons)

1 pound ground beef

1 (15-ounce) can diced tomatoes, drained

1 (26-ounce) jar spaghetti sauce or marinara sauce

2 to 4 tablespoons chopped fresh basil, plus minced fresh basil for garnish

1 teaspoon kosher salt, plus more to taste

2 teaspoons fresh oregano, or ½ teaspoon dried oregano

¼ teaspoon black pepper, plus more to taste

1 cup sour cream

2 cups grated fresh mozzarella cheese, plus more to taste

½ cup grated Parmesan cheese

1 Preheat the oven to 350°F. Spray a 9 × 13-inch baking dish with nonstick cooking spray.

2 Bring a large pot of water to a boil and cook the pasta according to the package directions until al dente. Drain and set aside.

3 In a large saucepan, heat the oil over medium heat. Add the onion and garlic and cook for 2 to 3 minutes, or until the onion is tender. Add the meat and cook until browned.

4 Drain any grease from the browned beef and stir in the tomatoes, spaghetti sauce, basil, salt, oregano, and pepper. Simmer for about 5 minutes.

5 Add the sour cream and pasta and stir until combined. Taste and adjust the seasoning. Transfer half the mixture to the prepared baking dish and top with 1 cup of the mozzarella. Pour the rest of the pasta mixture on top. Top the pasta with the remaining 1 cup mozzarella and the Parmesan. Add a little extra cheese if you like it really cheesy. Bake for 20 to 25 minutes, or until the cheese is bubbling. Top with fresh basil just before serving, if desired.

Assemble the dish and before baking, freeze the pasta in one 9 x 13-inch or two 8 x 8-inch aluminum pans. Cover the pans with aluminum foil and place them flat in large zip-top bags. When ready to cook, remove from the freezer and thaw on the counter for 1 to 2 hours. Preheat the oven to 350°F and bake for 35 to 40 minutes, or until the pasta is hot and bubbling.

HELPFUL ·TIP·

The sauce makes a great base for spaghetti (or just about any pasta). I omit the sour cream and mozzarella and then top the dish with the Parmesan.

cajun chicken pasta

SERVES
6

PREP
15 min

COOK
20 min

TOTAL
35 min

I have a weakness for pasta—there's something so comforting about it, and it is my go-to dish to order when eating out. This recipe re-creates the restaurant experience at home. The pasta is so delicious, simple to throw together, and incredibly versatile. You can change it up by mixing in your family's favorite meats and vegetables. The cream sauce will blend it all together and is the best part of the dish.

♥

1 Bring a large pot of water to a boil and cook the pasta according to the package directions. Drain the pasta, reserving ¼ cup of the pasta cooking water, and set aside in a large serving bowl.

2 While the pasta is cooking, in a large skillet, heat the oil over medium heat. Add the green onions and bell pepper and sauté for 3 to 5 minutes, until the pepper is tender. Add the garlic and cook for 1 minute more. Transfer the vegetables to a bowl.

3 In a small bowl, whisk together the flour and ¼ cup of the half-and-half until smooth. Pour the mixture into the pan and cook, stirring, for 1 to 2 minutes, or until it comes to a simmer. While stirring, slowly add the remaining half-and-half and whisk until smooth. Simmer for 3 to 5 minutes, or until the sauce begins to thicken slightly. Season with the Cajun seasoning and salt and black pepper to taste. Add the chicken, vegetables, and basil. Add more basil, if desired. If the sauce is too thick, add the reserved pasta cooking water in small increments until the desired consistency is reached.

4 Pour the sauce over the cooked pasta and stir until combined. Sprinkle with Parmesan and serve immediately.

VARIATION Try using different vegetables such as chopped broccoli or asparagus.

2 cups uncooked bow-tie (farfalle) pasta

1 to 2 tablespoons extra-virgin olive oil

¼ cup thinly sliced green onions

1 red bell pepper, chopped

2 garlic cloves, minced (1 teaspoon)

1 tablespoon all-purpose flour

2 cups half-and-half

½ teaspoon Cajun or Creole seasoning, plus more to taste

Salt and black pepper

2 cups shredded or cubed cooked chicken (I like to use a rotisserie chicken)

1 to 2 tablespoons minced fresh basil, or ½ teaspoon dried, plus more to taste

Freshly grated Parmesan cheese, for serving

SERVES
4–6

- - - - - -

PREP
20 min

- - - - - -

COOK
10 min

- - - - - -

TOTAL
30 min

STUFFED

bell peppers

These stuffed peppers are loaded with veggies and protein. That makes them completely healthy in my book! They are made in thirty minutes and make the perfect weeknight meal. My whole family loves them.

♥

4 large or 6 medium red or yellow bell peppers

¾ pound lean ground beef or turkey

1 cup chopped sweet onion

2 garlic cloves, minced (1 teaspoon)

1 (4-ounce) can diced green chiles

½ cup uncooked long-grain white rice or quinoa

1 (14-ounce) can petite diced tomatoes, with juice

1 (14-ounce) can black beans, drained and rinsed

1 cup frozen or canned corn

1 tablespoon chili powder, plus more to taste

½ tablespoon ground cumin

1¼ teaspoons kosher salt, plus more to taste

¼ teaspoon black pepper, plus more to taste

½ cup water or beef broth

½ to 1 cup shredded cheddar or Monterey Jack cheese

Optional toppings: sour cream, Favorite Homemade Salsa (page 158), chopped fresh cilantro, sliced green onions

1 Preheat the oven to 400°F.

2 Cut the tops off the peppers, removing as little as possible, and remove the seeds and ribs. Set aside.

3 In a large skillet, brown the meat over medium heat. Stir in the onion, garlic, and green chiles and cook until tender. Drain off any excess grease from the pan. Add the rice, tomatoes with their juice, black beans, corn, chili powder, cumin, salt, black pepper, and water. Bring to a boil, then cover the pan and reduce the heat to low. Cook for 8 to 10 minutes, or until the rice is tender. Taste for seasoning and add more chili powder, salt, or black pepper, if needed.

4 Meanwhile, bring a large pot of water to a boil. Place the peppers in the boiling water for 5 to 7 minutes to parcook them (this speeds up the cooking process). Drain and stand them upright in a 9 × 9-inch baking dish. (Alternatively, you can add 15 minutes to the baking time if you'd rather not parcook the peppers.)

5 Carefully spoon the meat mixture into the peppers. Sprinkle cheese on top and bake for 10 minutes, or until the cheese is bubbling. Add your favorite toppings and serve hot.

chicken cordon bleu pasta

This creamy casserole is a delightful twist on the traditional chicken cordon bleu. It takes a little bit of extra work, but will soon become a dish the whole family will enjoy. It is the ultimate comfort food and totally worth the extra calories. We like to serve this pasta with a large salad or steamed veggies.

SERVES
6

PREP
25 min

COOK
25 min

TOTAL
50 min

♥

1 Preheat the oven to 375°F. Butter a 9 × 9-inch baking dish.

2 Bring a large pot of water to a boil and cook the pasta, according to the package directions, until al dente. Drain the pasta, reserving ½ cup of the pasta cooking water, and transfer it to a bowl. Add the olive oil and toss to coat. Set aside.

3 While the pasta cooks, in a large saucepan, melt 4 tablespoons of the butter over medium heat. Add the onion and cook for 2 minutes. Reduce the heat to medium-low and add the garlic. Cook for 1 to 2 minutes, or until the onion is translucent. Add the cubes of cream cheese and allow them to melt. Very slowly whisk in the half-and-half and ½ cup of the Parmesan. Bring to a light simmer. Stir in 1 tablespoon of the parsley, the mustard, chicken, and ham. Season with salt and pepper and simmer for 5 minutes. Whisk in up to ¼ cup of the reserved pasta cooking water, if needed, to thin the sauce.

4 Add the noodles to the sauce and toss to coat, then transfer half the mixture to the prepared baking dish. Arrange the Swiss cheese on top, then add the remaining pasta on top of the cheese.

5 In a small microwave-safe bowl, melt the remaining 2 tablespoons butter in the microwave. Stir in the bread crumbs and the remaining 1 tablespoon parsley. Sprinkle the bread crumb mixture over the pasta, then sprinkle with the remaining ¾ cup Parmesan cheese. Add more if desired. Cover with aluminum foil and bake for 15 minutes. Remove the foil and bake for 10 minutes more, or until the top is lightly golden brown.

6 tablespoons (¾ stick) salted butter, plus more for the baking dish

2½ cups uncooked penne or ziti

1 tablespoon extra-virgin olive oil

½ cup chopped yellow onion

2 to 3 garlic cloves, minced (1 heaping teaspoon)

½ (8-ounce) package cream cheese, cut into cubes, at room temperature

1½ cups half-and-half

1¼ cups finely grated Parmesan cheese, plus more to taste

2 tablespoons finely chopped fresh parsley

1 teaspoon Dijon mustard

1½ cups diced cooked chicken

1 cup (¼-inch) pieces ham steak

Salt and black pepper

4 to 6 slices Swiss cheese

⅓ cup plain bread crumbs

NOTE *You can also skip the casserole and just mix the pasta and sauce together for a super-easy meal. This recipe also makes a great freezer meal.*

SERVES
6

PREP
20 min

COOK
13–15 min

TOTAL
33–35 min

chicken taquitos

Weekends were made for taquitos. They are the perfect appetizer or dinner, and are always devoured very quickly. Sour cream, salsa, chicken, and fresh cilantro come together in these amazing homemade taquitos. You'll never resort to store-bought ones again. Serve these up as a main dish or cut them in half for party appetizers. We top ours with Favorite Homemade Salsa (page 158) or The Best Guacamole (page 162).

½ (8-ounce) package cream cheese, at room temperature

¼ cup sour cream

¼ cup Favorite Homemade Salsa (page 158) or salsa of your choice (I like a chunky salsa with traditional flavors)

¼ teaspoon garlic powder

½ teaspoon ground cumin

¾ cup shredded Monterey Jack or pepper Jack cheese

¼ cup chopped fresh cilantro

2½ cups shredded cooked chicken (I like to use a rotisserie chicken)

Salt and black pepper

12 (6-inch) flour tortillas

Extra-virgin olive oil, for brushing

1 Preheat the oven to 400°F. Line a baking sheet with aluminum foil.

2 In a medium bowl, combine the cream cheese, sour cream, salsa, garlic powder, and cumin. Stir in the shredded cheese, cilantro, and chicken. Season with salt and pepper.

3 Place about 3 tablespoons of the cream cheese mixture in the center of a tortilla and roll up the tortilla. Place the tortilla seam side down on the prepared baking sheet. Repeat until all the tortillas are filled. Lightly brush the tortillas with olive oil and bake for 13 to 15 minutes, or until lightly browned. Serve while hot.

Place unbaked taquitos flat in a zip-top bag and freeze. When ready to eat, thaw, brush with olive oil, and bake according to the directions in the recipe.

enchiladas

My husband and I are big fans of enchiladas, and they were the first homemade meal I made when we got married. They are easy to make, freeze well, and make the perfect weeknight meal. This recipe is extremely versatile, and you can adjust the heat to your liking with the salsa and enchilada sauce. We serve them with rice, beans, chips, and salsa on the side.

SERVES
8

PREP
15 min

COOK
25–30 min

TOTAL
40–45 min

♥

1 Preheat the oven to 375°F. Pour one-quarter of the enchilada sauce into a 9 × 13-inch casserole dish and set aside.

2 In a large skillet, melt the butter over medium heat. Add the onion and green chiles and cook for 3 minutes. Add the salsa and cream cheese and stir with a spatula until the cream cheese has melted. Add the salt, cumin, and black pepper. Stir in ¼ cup of the cheddar cheese and the chicken.

3 Place about ¼ cup of the mixture in the center of a tortilla and roll up the tortilla. Place the tortilla seam side down on top of the enchilada sauce in the baking dish. Repeat with the remaining tortillas.

4 Top the tortillas with the remaining enchilada sauce and sprinkle the remaining cheddar and the pepper Jack cheeses on top.

5 Cover the pan with aluminum foil and bake for 15 to 20 minutes, or until the cheese has begun to melt. Remove the foil and bake for 10 minutes more, or until the cheese is bubbling. Remove from the oven and top with toppings of your choice. Enjoy while hot.

1 (10-ounce) can red or green enchilada sauce

2 tablespoons salted butter

½ cup chopped yellow onion

1 (4-ounce) can diced green chiles

¼ cup Favorite Homemade Salsa (page 158) or salsa of your choice (I like a chunky salsa with traditional flavors and a little kick)

½ (8-ounce) package cream cheese, cut into cubes

½ teaspoon kosher salt

¼ teaspoon ground cumin

¼ teaspoon black pepper

¾ cup shredded cheddar cheese

2½ cups shredded cooked chicken (I like to use a rotisserie chicken)

8 (8-inch) flour tortillas

1 cup shredded pepper Jack or Monterey Jack cheese

Optional toppings: chopped fresh cilantro, shredded lettuce, sour cream

FREEZER · TIP ·

Assemble the enchiladas and before baking, freeze the enchiladas in one 9 x 13-inch or two 8 x 8-inch aluminum pans. Cover the pans with aluminum foil and place them flat in large zip-top bags. When ready to cook, remove from the freezer and thaw on the counter for 1 to 2 hours. Preheat the oven to 350°F and bake for 35 to 40 minutes, or until the enchiladas are hot and bubbling.

cheesy bacon and chive macaroni

SERVES
4–6

PREP
15 min

COOK
15 min

TOTAL
30 min

The name says it all…bacon and cheese. Do I really need to say more? This recipe is so simple, but so good. It's known as gourmet macaroni in my house. The best part? You can make it in one pot in thirty minutes. This is the perfect meal for those crazy school nights. You can have dinner on the table in no time. For a lighter meal, you can also omit the bacon and ½ cup of the cheese.

- 1 tablespoon extra-virgin olive oil
- ½ cup chopped yellow onion
- 2 garlic cloves, minced (1 teaspoon)
- 2¼ cups chicken stock (one 16.9-ounce container)
- 1 cup canned diced tomatoes, drained
- 1 teaspoon ground mustard
- ¾ teaspoon kosher salt, plus more to taste
- ½ teaspoon Creole seasoning
- ¼ teaspoon black pepper, plus more to taste
- 2 cups elbow macaroni
- 1 cup shredded mild or sharp cheddar cheese
- 1 cup shredded Colby or Monterey Jack cheese
- 5 bacon slices, cooked crisp and crumbled (about ¼ cup)
- 2 tablespoons minced fresh chives

1 In a large saucepan, heat the oil over medium heat. Add the onion and cook for 2 minutes. Add the garlic and cook for 1 to 2 minutes more, or until the onion is translucent. Slowly pour in the stock and bring to a light simmer.

2 Stir in the tomatoes, mustard, salt, Creole seasoning, pepper, and macaroni. Bring to a boil, then cover the pot and reduce the heat to low. Cook for about 8 minutes, or until the noodles are cooked and the stock has mostly evaporated. Stir in the cheeses and top with the bacon and chives. Enjoy while it's hot!

HELPFUL ·TIP·

Precook your bacon to save time during meal prep. Line a baking sheet with foil and bake at 400°F for 15 to 20 minutes, or until crisp. If you're in a hurry, you can also use precooked bacon crumbles from the store.

FREEZER · TIP ·

I like to freeze half the sauce in a zip-top bag for another pizza night. You can also freeze half the dough as well, after it has risen. Place the dough in a zip-top bag and make sure all the air is out of the bag. When ready to use, just pull out the dough and thaw overnight in the refrigerator.

pizza night

One of my family's traditions is making homemade pizza together. My kids love rolling out the dough and choosing their toppings. This pizza dough has a nice crisp outside and great flavor. I share our favorite classic pizza sauce below, but you can also use a white sauce or pesto as your base. Then get creative with your toppings.

MAKES TWO

12-inch pizzas, to serve 8–10

- - - - - -

PREP
40 min

- - - - - -

COOK
20 min

- - - - - -

TOTAL
60 min

♥

1 **Make the pizza dough:** In a small bowl, mix the warm water, yeast, and sugar. Cover with plastic wrap and let sit for 5 minutes, or until it starts to foam.

2 In a large bowl or in the bowl of a stand mixer fitted with the dough hook, combine the yeast mixture, oil, honey, and salt. Add 1 cup of the flour and knead by hand or with the dough hook until combined. Add more flour, ¼ cup at a time, and knead until the dough is smooth, soft, and just a little bit sticky, but not to where the dough still sticks to the bowl. Knead for 3 to 5 minutes more. Roll the dough into a ball and rub a little oil around the dough. Place the dough in a clean bowl and cover with plastic wrap. Set aside for 20 minutes, or until the dough puffs up a bit. It doesn't need to rise much.

3 **Make the pizza sauce:** In a small bowl, whisk together the pizza sauce ingredients. Taste and adjust the seasoning. Set aside.

4 Preheat the oven to 450°F. Prep any toppings you'll be using.

5 Dust your work surface with flour. Turn out the dough, cut it in half, and then roll out each piece with a rolling pin or toss until the dough is about ¼ inch thick and 12 inches wide. (You can also divide the dough into quarters to make four 6-inch personal pizzas.)

6 Lightly brush a pizza stone or large baking sheet with oil. Place the dough on the stone or baking sheet. Spread sauce over the dough and add your favorite toppings.

7 Bake for 20 minutes, or until golden brown. For smaller pizzas, check them after about 12 minutes.

For the pizza dough

1 cup warm water (110°F)

1 tablespoon active dry yeast

1 tablespoon sugar

2 tablespoons extra-virgin olive oil

1½ tablespoons honey

1½ teaspoons table salt or fine sea salt

2½ to 3 cups all-purpose flour

For the pizza sauce

1 (8-ounce) can tomato sauce

1 tablespoon chopped fresh basil, or ½ teaspoon dried basil

1 teaspoon ground oregano

1 garlic clove, minced (½ teaspoon)

¼ teaspoon fine sea salt or table salt, plus more to taste

⅛ teaspoon black pepper, plus more to taste

Flour, for dusting

Olive oil, for brushing

Optional toppings: shredded or sliced mozzarella, sliced tomatoes, fresh basil, pepperoni, sliced bell peppers, olives, sliced onion, mushrooms, Canadian bacon, pineapple, jalapeños

slow cook it, baby!

♥

*Cooking is like love. It should be entered
into with abandon or not at all.*

—HARRIET VAN HORNE

We all have those crazy days where there is absolutely no time to
make dinner. That's where my best friend, the slow cooker,
comes in handy. Spend fifteen minutes in the morning prepping
and have dinner done by the time you get home.

RECIPES

SERVES
6—8

PREP
10 min

COOK
3—4 hours

TOTAL
approx
4 hours

SHREDDED

chicken tacos

This recipe is great for when you need to put together something fast in the morning. The meat is super juicy, full of flavor, and tender, and literally falls apart by the time it is done cooking. The leftover chicken also freezes well for a night when you need a quick meal.

6 large boneless, skinless chicken breasts

¾ cup chicken broth

3 garlic cloves, minced (1½ teaspoons)

1 (1-ounce) packet ranch seasoning mix (such as Hidden Valley)

2 teaspoons chili powder

2 teaspoons ground cumin

Juice of 1 lime

Kosher salt and black pepper

8 (6-inch) flour or corn tortillas

Optional toppings: shredded lettuce, shredded cheese, sautéed onions and peppers, Favorite Homemade Salsa (page 158), sour cream, The Best Guacamole (page 162)

1 Place the chicken breasts in a slow cooker and pour in the chicken broth. Add the garlic, ranch mix, chili powder, and cumin on top of the chicken and stir. Cover and cook on High for 3 to 4 hours, or until the meat easily shreds with a fork.

2 Shred the chicken and remove any excess fat. Return the meat to the slow cooker. Stir in the lime juice and salt and pepper to taste. Turn the slow cooker to Warm until ready to serve.

3 Serve the chicken in tortillas with your favorite toppings.

HELPFUL
·TIP·

I also love to use this recipe when I am making a big batch of plain shredded chicken for the week. I keep cooked chicken on hand for salads: I follow this recipe, but I omit the ranch seasoning, chili powder, cumin, and lime. You can then store the chicken to use in meals throughout the week or freeze in a zip-top bag for later use.

teriyaki chicken

SERVES
6

PREP
10 min

COOK
4–6 hours

TOTAL
approx
6 hours

A meal that can be prepped in ten minutes is priceless when you've got a busy day ahead. This teriyaki chicken is just that and the sweet sauce is absolutely divine. This recipe tastes much better than takeout and is loved by all.

♥

1 Place the chicken in a slow cooker and pour in ¼ cup water. Set the heat to Low. In a medium bowl, whisk together ¼ cup water and the cornstarch, then whisk in the granulated sugar, brown sugar, soy sauce, vinegar, garlic, ginger, and pepper.

2 Pour the sauce over the chicken, cover, and cook on Low for 4 to 6 hours, or until the meat shreds easily with a fork. Remove any fat and shred the chicken. Return the chicken to the slow cooker and stir to coat with the sauce. Turn the slow cooker to Warm until ready to serve. Plate the chicken with cooked rice and steamed vegetables. Garnish with sesame seeds and green onions, if desired.

NOTE *If using frozen chicken, you may need to add an extra hour to the cooking time.*

1½ to 2 pounds boneless, skinless chicken breasts

2 tablespoons cornstarch

½ cup granulated sugar

¼ cup packed light brown sugar

½ cup lite soy sauce

½ cup apple cider vinegar

3 garlic cloves, minced (1½ teaspoons)

1 teaspoon ground ginger

½ teaspoon black pepper, plus more to taste

4 to 6 cups cooked rice, for serving

Steamed vegetables (like broccoli, carrots, snap peas), for serving

Sesame seeds and sliced green onions, for garnish (optional)

The leftover chicken freezes really well. Let the chicken cool and then place in a zip-top bag.

SERVES
8–10

PREP
10 min

COOK
2–3 hours

TOTAL
approx
3 hours

SWEET-AND-SOUR

meatballs

My grandpa has been making these meatballs for as long as I can remember. My siblings and I always loved them growing up, and my sister even talked him into making them as an appetizer at her wedding. They were a huge hit!

The best part about these meatballs is, no one would ever know they were so simple to make. These make great appetizers, but you can also serve them over sticky rice for a more filling main dish.

♥

1 cup barbecue sauce (I like Sweet Baby Ray's)

¾ cup grape jelly

2 teaspoons Worcestershire sauce

1 garlic clove, minced (½ teaspoon)

1 (about 26-ounce) bag frozen fully cooked Italian-style dinner-size meatballs

Salt and black pepper

Cooked rice, for serving (optional)

1 Combine the barbecue sauce, jelly, Worcestershire sauce, and garlic in a slow cooker set on Low. Stir the sauce until combined. Add the meatballs and stir until they are coated with the sauce. Cover and cook on Low for 2 to 3 hours, or until fully cooked. Stir the meatballs and turn the slow cooker to Warm until ready to serve. Season with salt and pepper.

2 Enjoy as an appetizer or serve over rice for a main dish.

VARIATION You can also substitute 2 (14-ounce) packages of mini sausages (little smokies) for the meatballs and serve with toothpicks for a fun appetizer.

CHICKEN

burrito bowls

These burrito bowls are a simplified, homemade version of ones
you'll find at popular Mexican restaurants. They are fresh, full of flavor,
customizable, and so easy to make. The toppings and cilantro lime rice are
what make these burrito bowls, so load up!

SERVES
4–6

PREP
10 min

COOK
4–6 hours

TOTAL
approx
6 hours

♥

1 Place the chicken in a slow cooker and pour the salsa and
tomatoes over the chicken. Add the chili powder, cumin,
garlic, lime juice, and black beans and stir. Cover and cook on
Low for 4 to 6 hours, or until the chicken is tender. Remove
the chicken and cut into strips or shred. Return the chicken
to the slow cooker and stir. Season with salt and pepper. Turn
the slow cooker to Warm until ready to serve.

2 Layer the cilantro rice and chicken mixture in
individual bowls and serve with your favorite toppings.

4 boneless, skinless chicken breasts
(about 1½ pounds)

1 cup Favorite Homemade Salsa
(page 158) or store-bought salsa

1½ teaspoons chili powder

1 teaspoon ground cumin

2 garlic cloves, minced (1 teaspoon)

Juice of 1 lime

1 (15-ounce) can black beans,
drained and rinsed

1 (10-ounce) can diced tomatoes
with green chiles

Salt and black pepper

Cilantro Lime Rice (page 73), for
serving

Optional toppings: shredded
cheddar cheese, shredded
lettuce, sliced avocados, sour
cream, pico de gallo, tortilla
strips, chopped fresh cilantro

SERVES
6–8

PREP
20 min

COOK
up to
8 hours

TOTAL
approx
8 hours

SWEET PORK

hawaiian haystacks

We can't get enough of these Hawaiian haystacks in my house. The meat is cooked in the slow cooker to make dinner a breeze. This version is made with sweet pork and completely customizable with all your favorite toppings; the more, the better, in my opinion! I like to layer the rice and meat, and then add pineapple, green onions, shredded cheese, and chow mein noodles for extra crunch. The leftover meat also makes great pulled pork sandwiches or burritos.

♥

2 to 3 pounds pork tenderloin

1 to 2 teaspoons Himalayan pink salt

¼ teaspoon black pepper

1 cup red enchilada sauce

1 cup light brown sugar

1 garlic clove, minced (½ teaspoon)

2 tablespoons pineapple juice (from the can of pineapple)

Cooked rice, for serving

Canned pineapple chunks, for serving

Chopped green onions, for serving

Chow mein noodles, for serving

Optional toppings: canned mandarin oranges, sliced olives, chopped red bell peppers, shredded cheese, cashews

1 Place the pork and ¼ cup water in a slow cooker. Pierce the meat with a fork several times and then sprinkle with the salt and pepper. Cover and cook on High for 4 to 6 hours or Low for 7 to 8 hours, or until the meat begins to fall apart.

2 In a small saucepan, combine the enchilada sauce, brown sugar, garlic, and pineapple juice. Bring to a light boil over medium heat, stirring continuously. Reduce the heat to low and simmer for 3 to 5 minutes, or until the sauce begins to thicken.

3 Remove the pork from the slow cooker and shred the meat, discarding the fat. Return the shredded pork to the slow cooker and add the sauce. Turn the slow cooker to Warm until ready to serve.

4 Serve the sweet pork over rice and top with pineapple, green onions, and chow mein noodles. Add additional toppings, if desired.

shredded beef

I absolutely love all the juicy flavors in this green chile shredded beef.
My family enjoys this recipe for tacos and burritos. The leftovers
freeze great and also make great enchiladas. For enchiladas, place the meat in
tortillas, roll them up, and pour green enchilada sauce on top with
shredded cheese. Done and done!

SERVES
8

PREP
15 min

COOK
6–8 hours

TOTAL
approx
8 hours

1 Place the chuck roast in a slow cooker. Pour in the broth and sprinkle the salt and taco seasoning over the roast.

2 Add the salsa, 1 can of the green chiles, and the onion on top of the roast. Cover and cook on Low for 6 to 8 hours, or until the meat easily shreds.

3 Remove the roast from the pan and discard any excess fat. Shred the meat with two forks and then return it to the slow cooker with the remaining 1 can green chiles. Season to taste with salt and black pepper. Turn the slow cooker to Warm until ready to serve.

4 Place the shredded beef inside taco shells or tortillas and add your favorite toppings.

4 to 5 pounds boneless beef chuck roast

¼ cup beef broth or water

½ teaspoon kosher salt, plus more to taste

1½ tablespoons taco seasoning

1 (16-ounce) jar salsa verde

2 (4.5-ounce) cans diced green chiles

¾ cup chopped yellow onion

Black pepper

Taco shells or tortillas, for serving

Green enchilada sauce, for serving (optional)

Optional toppings: shredded cheese, shredded lettuce, cherry tomatoes, pico de gallo, cilantro, sour cream

SERVES
6
- - - - - -
PREP
15 min
- - - - - -
COOK
4 hours
- - - - - -
TOTAL
4 hours
15 min

chicken tortilla soup

I triple love this chicken tortilla soup. It is so easy to make and the
ideal meal for busy weeknights. This will be one of your new go-to recipes!
I like to top mine with lots of freshly grated cheese, fresh cilantro,
tortilla strips, avocado slices, and a lime wedge.

♥

- 4 large boneless, skinless chicken breasts
- 3 (14-ounce) cans chicken broth
- 2 teaspoons chili powder
- ½ teaspoon kosher salt, plus more to taste
- 2 (15-ounce) cans black beans, drained and rinsed
- 1 (15-ounce) can corn, drained
- 1 (14.5-ounce) can diced tomatoes, with juice
- 1 (4-ounce) can diced green chiles
- ½ cup chopped onion
- ½ cup chopped red bell pepper
- ¼ cup chopped fresh cilantro
- Juice of ½ lime
- 2 tablespoons taco seasoning
- 2 garlic cloves, minced (1 teaspoon)
- ½ teaspoon ground cumin
- Black pepper
- Tortilla strips or crushed tortilla chips
- Optional toppings: shredded cheese, pico de gallo, avocado, sour cream

1 Place the chicken in a slow cooker and pour in the broth. Sprinkle the chili powder and salt on top. Add the black beans, corn, tomatoes with their juice, green chiles, onion, bell pepper, and cilantro and stir. Sprinkle lime juice, taco seasoning, garlic, and cumin over the top and stir. Cover and cook on High for 3 to 4 hours or on Low for 6 to 8 hours.

2 Remove the chicken and shred or cut it into bite-size pieces. Return the chicken to the slow cooker and cook on Low for 30 minutes more. Season with salt and black pepper.

3 Just before serving, add tortilla strips. You can also add cheese, pico de gallo, avocado, and sour cream, if desired.

pot roast & homemade gravy

SERVES
6–8

PREP
20 min

COOK
6 hours

TOTAL
6 hours
20 min

One of my favorite childhood memories is of sitting around the table every Sunday with my family. We always knew it was going to be a good dinner when Mom put the pot roast in the oven before church. This pot roast is a classic, never-fail recipe. When it's done, it will be incredibly juicy and will literally fall apart. The homemade gravy is full of flavor and tastes amazing over the roast and the vegetables or when served with the Creamiest Mashed Potatoes (page 70).

♥

2 tablespoons extra-virgin olive oil

3½ pounds boneless beef chuck pot roast

Kosher salt and black pepper

1½ to 2 cups beef broth

1 large onion, sliced

4 to 5 garlic cloves, minced (2 to 2½ teaspoons)

2 sprigs fresh rosemary

1 pound carrots, cut into 2-inch pieces (optional)

2 pounds red potatoes, halved (optional)

3 tablespoons unsalted butter

3 tablespoons all-purpose flour

1 In a large skillet, heat the oil over medium heat. Liberally season the roast with salt and pepper, then place in the skillet. Brown the meat on all sides in the hot oil, then transfer to a slow cooker. Pour the broth over the roast.

2 Place the onion and garlic in the skillet and cook for 2 to 3 minutes, or until golden brown. Transfer the onion and garlic to the slow cooker on top of the roast and add the rosemary.

3 If desired, add the carrots and potatoes, then season the vegetables with salt and pepper.

4 Cover and cook on Low for 6 to 8 hours, or until the meat is tender.

5 Remove and discard the rosemary sprigs. Transfer the roast and vegetables to a serving tray and cover with aluminum foil. Pour the liquid from the slow cooker into a fat separator or through a fine-mesh strainer into a bowl. You should end up with 2 to 3 cups of liquid.

6 In a large saucepan, melt the butter over medium heat. Slowly whisk in the flour and stir until the mixture has thickened. Slowly whisk in the pot roast cooking liquid and bring to a light simmer. Cook until the gravy has thickened, 3 to 5 minutes. Season with salt and pepper.

7 Enjoy the gravy over the roast, potatoes, and carrots.

FROM MY KITCHEN TO YOURS

One of the best things you can give someone after they've
come home from the hospital is a homemade meal.

When I bring someone dinner, I like to pack everything in disposable containers. This way, they don't have to worry about getting dishes washed and back to me. I also like to include paper plates and utensils. Fewer dishes is always a good thing, right?

Here are a few other things I like to include with the meal: fresh fruit and veggies, dessert, and small indulgences like a magazine and chocolate.

Here are my favorite meals to bring to others: One-Pot Taco Soup (page 105), Shredded Chicken Tacos and toppings (page 140), and Cheesy Baked Ziti (page 122). They are all easy to prepare in aluminum pans, and are always crowd-pleasers.

party snacks
& drinks

♥

First we eat. Then we do everything else.

—M.F.K. FISHER

These delicious drinks and party snacks are sure to win over your guests. Whip up these delicious recipes for parties, showers, football games, or girls' nights out.

-------------------- RECIPES --------------------

MAKES
5 CUPS

PREP
10 min

CHILL
30 min

TOTAL
40 min

homemade salsa

Being born and raised in Arizona, I have become a bit of a salsa snob. I grew up eating chips and salsa, and nothing compares to homemade salsa. I make this recipe almost weekly because it is so easy to whip up and tastes way better than anything I can find in the store. This salsa tastes amazing with tortilla chips or on top of just about any Mexican dish.

♥

2 (15-ounce) cans diced tomatoes, with juice

1 (4-ounce) can diced green chiles

½ cup chopped fresh cilantro, plus more to taste

¼ cup finely chopped yellow onion

Juice of 1 lime

1 garlic clove, minced (½ teaspoon)

1 teaspoon kosher salt, plus more to taste

1 teaspoon sugar

½ teaspoon ground cumin

½ to 1 jalapeño, finely chopped (optional)

1 Combine all the ingredients in a food processor or blender. Pulse 5 to 7 times, or until everything is evenly blended but not pureed.

2 Taste the salsa and add up to ¼ cup more cilantro and ¼ teaspoon more salt, if needed. For more spice, add the whole jalapeño.

3 Transfer to a bowl, cover, and refrigerate until ready to serve. I like to refrigerate this salsa at least 30 minutes before serving to help marry the flavors.

NOTE *If you like a chunkier salsa, drain the liquid from the tomatoes and pulse only a couple of times.*

Make sure to taste each recipe as you go. Everyone has different taste buds, so adjust accordingly; add salt and pepper a bit at a time until the dish suits your taste. Once you begin feeling more comfortable in the kitchen, try playing with different herbs and spices.

grilled corn and bean salsa

I have been known to eat an entire bowl of this salsa in one sitting.
It is seriously addictive, and always a big hit at parties. It tastes great served
with tortilla or pita chips. We also love to serve this salsa on top
of salads, quesadillas, nachos, and Shredded Chicken Tacos (page 140). Pretty
much everything!

SERVES
8

PREP
20 min

COOK
10 min

CHILL
20 min

TOTAL
50 min

♥

1 Heat a grill to medium-high. Brush the corn with the oil and season with salt and black pepper. Grill the corn, rotating it every 3 minutes to prevent it from charring too much on one side, for about 10 minutes, or until the corn is evenly cooked and speckled lightly with charred spots. Remove from the grill and let cool. Use a knife or corn cutter to remove the corn kernels.

2 While the corn is cooking, in a medium bowl, combine the black beans, black-eyed peas, bell pepper, onion, cilantro, tomatoes, jalapeño (if using), teaspoon of salt, and lime juice. Add the corn and gently fold in the avocado. Season with salt and pepper. Cover and refrigerate for 20 minutes, or until ready to serve.

3 Enjoy with tortilla chips.

2 large ears corn, husked

1 tablespoon extra-virgin olive oil

1 teaspoon kosher salt, plus more for seasoning

Black pepper

1 (15-ounce) can black beans, drained and rinsed

1 (15-ounce) can black-eyed peas, drained and rinsed

½ cup chopped red bell pepper

¼ cup finely chopped red onion

¾ cup chopped fresh cilantro

4 Roma (plum) tomatoes, finely chopped

½ jalapeño, finely chopped (optional)

Juice of 1 lime, plus lime wedges for serving

2 avocados, pitted, peeled, and diced

Tortilla or pita chips, for serving

HELPFUL TIP

If fresh corn is not in season, feel free to substitute 1 (15-ounce) can corn, drained.

SERVES
8–10

PREP
15 min

TOTAL
15 min

THE BEST

guacamole

Does guacamole even need an introduction? I love this recipe because it is so simple and delicious. It's another dip I could eat in one sitting, any time of day. The trick to perfecting guacamole is using good, ripe avocados. This recipe has been a huge hit with friends and family over the years and is hands-down my favorite way to make guacamole.

♥

3 ripe Hass avocados, pitted and peeled

Juice of 1 lime

¼ cup finely chopped red onion

2 to 3 tablespoons Favorite Homemade Salsa (page 158), or 1 Roma (plum) tomato, finely diced

1 garlic clove, minced (½ teaspoon)

¼ cup chopped fresh cilantro

½ jalapeño, finely chopped (optional)

½ teaspoon kosher salt, plus more to taste

Dash of black pepper, plus more to taste

Tortilla chips, for serving

1 In a medium bowl, mash together the avocado and lime juice with a fork or potato masher until they reach the desired consistency. Stir in the onion, salsa, garlic, cilantro, jalapeño, salt, and pepper. Taste and add more salt and pepper, if desired. Cover tightly with plastic wrap and refrigerate until ready to serve.

2 Enjoy with fresh tortilla chips or your favorite Mexican dish.

hot spinach artichoke dip

This recipe is a classic that can be prepped in ten minutes or less. It is loaded with three different kinds of cheese and all kinds of yummy, creamy flavors. It is my go-to dish to take to a party and can easily be made the night before. Just place the filling in the refrigerator and bake right before the party.

SERVES
8–10

PREP
10 min

COOK
20–25 min

TOTAL
30–35 min

♥

1 Preheat the oven to 400°F.

2 In a medium bowl, using a hand mixer, beat the cream cheese until smooth. Stir in the sour cream, mayonnaise, ¾ cup of the mozzarella, the Parmesan, garlic powder, parsley, salt, and pepper. Chop the artichokes into chunky pieces. Be careful to remove any pieces that may still have the prickly center. Fold the artichoke hearts, green chiles (if using), and spinach into the cream cheese mixture. At this point, the mixture can be refrigerated until ready to bake, up to overnight.

3 When ready to bake, place the mixture in a 9-inch pie dish or skillet. Top with the remaining ¼ cup mozzarella and bake for 20 to 25 minutes, or until bubbling.

4 Serve hot, with your favorite crostini, tortilla chips, or crackers.

NOTE *We also love to make this dip in the slow cooker. Simply stir together all the ingredients right in the bowl of the slow cooker and cook on High for 30 minutes, or until hot. Stir, and then turn the slow cooker to Warm until ready to serve.*

1 (8-ounce) package cream cheese, at room temperature

¼ cup sour cream

¼ cup mayonnaise

1 cup shredded mozzarella cheese

½ cup grated Parmesan cheese

½ teaspoon garlic powder

½ teaspoon dried parsley flakes

¼ teaspoon fine sea salt, plus more to taste

¼ teaspoon black pepper, plus more to taste

1 (10-ounce) can artichoke hearts (about 1 cup), drained

¼ cup canned diced green chiles, drained (optional)

1½ to 2 cups fresh chopped spinach

Crostini, tortilla chips, or crackers, for serving

SERVES
6

- - - - -

PREP
10 min

- - - - -

COOK
10 min

- - - - -

TOTAL
20 min

GARDEN FRESH

bruschetta

I adore fresh bruschetta in the summertime. It's light and refreshing, and if you have fresh tomatoes, it really can't be beat. My kids love going out to our garden and picking the ripe tomatoes and basil for this recipe. This is the perfect appetizer to make when you have friends coming over and want to make something quick!

♥

1½ cups finely chopped Roma (plum) tomatoes (about 5)

2 tablespoons extra-virgin olive oil

3 garlic cloves: 1 minced, 2 halved

1 tablespoon balsamic vinegar

3 tablespoons fresh basil leaves, cut into chiffonade

1 to 2 tablespoons chopped fresh oregano

Salt and black pepper

2 tablespoons salted butter

1 French Baguette (page 57), cut into ¾-inch slices

¼ cup grated Parmesan or crumbled feta cheese (optional)

1 In a medium bowl, combine the tomatoes, oil, minced garlic, vinegar, basil, oregano, and salt and pepper to taste. Set aside to marinate for 10 minutes.

2 In a large skillet or grill pan, melt the butter over medium heat. Set the bread in the pan. Cook for 2 to 3 minutes per side, or until slightly browned. Lightly rub the garlic halves over the bread and set aside to cool slightly. Alternatively, broil in the oven until golden brown.

3 Spoon about 2 tablespoons of the tomato mixture on top of each slice. Sprinkle the cheese on top, if desired.

VARIATION We also love roasted bruschetta. Top with shredded mozzarella after the tomatoes have been set on the bread and broil for 3 to 5 minutes, or until lightly browned.

DIY VASE

PROJECT TIME: 30 MIN

Widemouthed mason jar
Cardboard or newspaper
Spray paint

1 Working outside or in a well-ventilated area, place the jar on top of the cardboard with the opening of the jar facing down. Holding the can at least 10 inches away, apply a thin coat of spray paint. Allow the paint to dry for 10 minutes and then add another thin coat. Apply a third coat if the jar was not fully covered. Allow the vase to dry and then fill with water and fresh flowers.

2 This makes a great gift, too. Just tie it with ribbon and a tag. You can photocopy a tag from page 254, or download a printable version from my website at www.iheartnaptime.net /book-template.

SERVES
10–12

PREP
15 min

CHILL
20–30 min

TOTAL
35–45 min

DRESSED-UP

cheese ball

This cheese ball is the perfect appetizer to take to a holiday gathering, and it can be prepared the day ahead. The pineapple adds a touch of sweetness and it tastes great served with a variety of crackers and vegetables. For a more savory cheese ball, you can omit the pineapple and add a dash of hot sauce.

♥

1½ (8-ounce) packages cream cheese, at room temperature

¼ cup sour cream

¾ cup shredded cheddar cheese

¼ cup thinly sliced green onions

1 tablespoon ranch seasoning mix (such as Hidden Valley)

½ cup crushed drained pineapple

¾ cup pecans, coarsely chopped

Crackers, crostini, or chips, for serving

1 In a medium bowl, using a hand mixer, beat together the cream cheese and sour cream until smooth. Stir in the cheddar, green onions, and ranch seasoning. Gently fold in the pineapple. Place the mixture on a large piece of plastic wrap and form it into a ball or log. Place in the freezer for 20 to 30 minutes.

2 Spread the pecans on a plate. Remove the cheese ball from the plastic wrap and carefully roll it in the pecans until well coated. Press the pecans lightly into the cheese ball to help them adhere. Store in an airtight container for up to 3 days.

3 Place the cheese ball on a platter with crackers and serve at room temperature.

MAKES
36
pretzel bites

- - - - - -

PREP
25 min

- - - - - -

COOK
8–10 min

- - - - - -

REST
20 min

- - - - - -

TOTAL
53–55 min

HOT BUTTERED

soft pretzel bites

To say I'm in love with these would be a big understatement. They are warm, soft, and buttery and much better than anything you can buy at the store, plus much cheaper. They do require a little extra effort, but are so very worth it. Dip them into your favorite cheese sauce for a savory snack, or add cinnamon sugar on top for a sweet dessert!

- ♥ -

1 cup warm water (110°F)

1 (¼-ounce) packet active dry yeast (2¼ teaspoons)

2¼ to 3 cups all-purpose flour, plus more for dusting

2 teaspoons granulated sugar

1¼ teaspoons table salt or fine sea salt

1½ cups hot water

3 tablespoons baking soda

Coarse salt, for topping (optional)

4 tablespoons (½ stick) unsalted butter, melted

1 In a small bowl, stir together the warm water and yeast. Cover with plastic wrap and let sit for 3 to 5 minutes, or until it begins to foam.

2 In a large bowl or in the bowl of a stand mixer fitted with the dough hook, combine ½ cup of the flour, the sugar, and the table salt. Pour the yeast mixture over the top and stir by hand or with the dough hook. Continue to add flour, ¼ cup at a time, stirring continuously, until the dough is soft and no longer sticking to the sides. (You may not need to use all the flour.) Cover the bowl with plastic wrap and set aside for 15 to 20 minutes, or until it begins to rise.

3 Preheat the oven to 450°F. Line two baking sheets with silicone baking mats or parchment paper.

4 Turn out the dough onto a floured surface and separate it into six equal sections. Roll each piece into a rope about 1 inch thick and 8 inches long. Using a sharp knife, cut each rope into six 1- to 2-inch pieces. You should have 36 pieces total.

5 Combine the hot water and baking soda in a shallow bowl. Line a plate with a paper towel. Place the pretzel bites, 6 at a time, into the baking soda water and allow them to soak for 30 seconds. Remove the bites with a slotted spoon and place on the paper towel–lined plate. Once all the pretzels have been dipped, carefully transfer them to the prepared baking sheets. Let rest for 5 minutes. Sprinkle the coarse salt on top of the pretzels, if desired.

6 Bake for 8 to 10 minutes, or until golden brown. Brush the tops with melted butter.

7 The pretzel bites taste best warm right out of the oven, but they will keep in an airtight container at room temperature for up to 2 days. Warm them for 10 seconds in the microwave before serving.

VARIATION For a sweeter pretzel bite, bake the pretzels without the coarse salt topping. When they come out of the oven, roll them in melted butter and then roll the tops and sides in cinnamon sugar (½ cup granulated sugar combined with 2 tablespoons ground cinnamon). Serve warm.

chicken salad sandwiches

SERVES
6–8

PREP
15 min

CHILL
15 min

TOTAL
30 min

Chicken salad sandwiches are one of my go-to dishes to make for a bridal shower or baby shower—everyone loves them. I've tried some that are boring and flavorless, but this recipe is far from that. The combination of textures and flavors is irresistible. Pile it high on top of a sandwich, stuff it into pita pockets, or spread it on top of crackers for a yummy snack.

♥

1 In a large bowl, stir together the mayonnaise, lemon juice, and sour cream. Stir in the green onions, brown sugar, dill, salt, garlic powder, and pepper until combined.

2 Stir in the celery, grapes, and cashews until evenly coated. Finally, stir in the chicken. Refrigerate for at least 15 minutes before serving. Taste and add more dill, salt, and pepper, if needed.

3 Serve the mixture on the rolls and top with fresh lettuce.

HELPFUL · TIP ·

This mixture is best served the day it's made. You may also make it the night before; however, don't put the mixture on the rolls until just before serving.

¼ cup mayonnaise

Juice of ½ lemon

2 to 3 tablespoons sour cream or plain yogurt

2 tablespoons thinly sliced green onions

1½ teaspoons light brown sugar

2 teaspoons minced fresh dill, plus more to taste

¼ teaspoon kosher salt, plus more to taste

¼ teaspoon garlic powder

⅛ teaspoon black pepper, plus more to taste

1 cup chopped celery

1 cup halved red grapes

¼ cup cashews, chopped, or slivered almonds

3 cups chopped cooked chicken (I like to use a rotisserie chicken)

8 ciabatta or croissant rolls

Green-leaf lettuce, for garnish

SERVES
8–10

PREP
10 min

TOTAL
10 min

CREAMY

fruit dip

*This fruit dip is so creamy and easy to whip up. Every time
I take this to a party, it is gone within minutes. It pairs best with strawberries,
bananas, and grapes. For an elegant presentation
when serving to guests, skewer the fruit.*

♥

1 (8-ounce) package cream cheese,
    at room temperature

1 (7-ounce) tub marshmallow crème
    (such as Fluff)

Zest of ½ orange

1 tablespoon fresh orange juice

1 cup frozen nondairy whipped
    topping, at room temperature

Fresh fruit, such as strawberries,
    bananas, apples, and grapes, cut
    into bite-size pieces, for dipping

1 In a medium bowl, using a hand mixer, beat the cream
cheese until smooth. Add the marshmallow crème,
orange zest, and orange juice. Mix just until combined, then
fold in the nondairy whipped topping. Cover and refrigerate
until ready to serve.

2 Serve with the fresh fruit for dipping.

VARIATION Substitute strawberry cream cheese for the cream
cheese and lemon zest and juice for the orange for a yummy twist.

FRESH
strawberry lemonade

There's nothing better than fresh-squeezed strawberry lemonade, especially in the summer. I still remember making a big batch of lemonade as a little girl. I would set up shop in the Arizona sun and sell it to everyone who drove by. Now my kids love to sell lemonade and doughnuts. We live in a cul-de-sac, so we don't get much traffic, but they are always happy with the couple of bucks they earn. This strawberry lemonade is so simple to make and very refreshing on a hot summer day.

MAKES
10
cups

PREP
15 min

COOK
7 min

CHILL
20 min

TOTAL
42 min

♥

1 Zest one of the lemons and set the zest aside. Juice all 8 lemons. You should have 1¼ cups juice.

2 In a medium saucepan, bring 3 cups water to a light simmer over medium heat. Slowly stir in 1½ cups of the sugar and simmer for 3 to 5 minutes, or until the sugar has dissolved. Remove from the heat and pour the sugar-water into a pitcher. Let cool for about 10 minutes. Stir in 4 cups cold water and the lemon juice. Refrigerate until the mixture has fully cooled.

3 In a blender, combine the strawberries, lemon zest, the remaining 2 tablespoons sugar, and ½ cup water. Blend on high until the strawberries are pureed. If desired, strain the strawberry mixture through a fine-mesh strainer into a bowl to remove the seeds. (I like to keep some of the seeds in my lemonade, so I usually strain only half the mixture and add the rest as is.)

4 Add the strawberry puree to the lemonade and stir until well combined. Taste the lemonade; if it's too sweet, add another cup of cold water. Alternatively, if you'd like it a little sweeter, stir in 1 to 2 tablespoons more sugar. Refrigerate until ready to serve.

5 Serve the lemonade in glasses garnished with fresh lemon slices, if desired.

8 medium lemons

7½ to 8½ cups water

1½ cups plus 2 tablespoons sugar, plus more as needed

1½ to 2 cups hulled and halved strawberries

Lemon slices, for garnish

MAKES
14
cups

- - - - -

PREP
10 min

- - - - -

TOTAL
10 min

pineapple punch

This punch was made for parties, and especially for my little girl
who loves anything pink. It is so easy, and makes the yummiest and prettiest
punch for any occasion! You can also use rainbow sherbet in
place of the raspberry for a tasty twist.

♥

1 (2-liter) bottle lemon-lime soda

4 cups pineapple juice

1 quart raspberry sherbet

½ cup frozen raspberries

In a large punch bowl or pitcher, mix the lemon-lime soda
and pineapple juice. Scoop the raspberry sherbet into the
bowl and stir together. Top with the frozen raspberries.
Enjoy while cold!

This recipe is easy to cut in half if you're
making it for a smaller crowd. It's also very
easy to double for a larger crowd.

smoothie

SERVES
2–4

PREP
5 min

TOTAL
5 min

I love nothing more than relaxing on the beach. Add a fresh piña colada and a good book, and I'm in absolute heaven. We love making piña colada smoothies at home, especially when we're dreaming of being on the beach. This recipe is so easy to whip up and is a real sweet treat.

♥

1 In a blender, combine the milk, cream of coconut, and vanilla. Make sure to stir the cream of coconut before measuring. Add the sugar and frozen pineapple. Blend on high until smooth. Add the ice and blend until the desired consistency is reached. Taste and add more sugar, if needed.

2 Pour into glasses, garnish with fresh pineapple slices, if desired, and enjoy!

1 cup low-fat milk

¼ cup cream of coconut (I prefer Coco Lopez)

½ teaspoon vanilla extract

1 tablespoon sugar, plus more as needed

2 cups frozen pineapple

1 cup ice

Fresh pineapple slices, for garnish (optional)

SERVES
4

PREP
5 min

COOK
10 min

TOTAL
15 min

CREAMY

hot chocolate

In the winter months, all I want are a few things: a cozy blanket, fuzzy socks, and a warm glass of hot chocolate in my hand. Behold, my favorite winter drink: creamy, rich hot chocolate, topped with whipped cream, marshmallows, and extra chocolate. We love to make this recipe and snuggle up on the couch whenever a big snowstorm comes in. This recipe doubles easily to serve a crowd.

♥

3 cups low-fat milk

1 cup heavy cream

1 cup semisweet chocolate chips

¼ cup sugar

⅛ teaspoon fine sea salt

½ teaspoon vanilla extract

Pinch of ground cinnamon (optional)

Whipped cream and mini marshmallows, for serving (optional)

1 In a medium saucepan, combine the milk, heavy cream, and chocolate chips and heat over medium-low heat, whisking frequently, until the mixture is smooth and the chocolate has melted. Reduce the heat to low and whisk in the sugar and salt. Cook for 3 minutes more, or until the sugar has dissolved and the hot chocolate is warm. Remove from the heat and stir in the vanilla and cinnamon, if desired. Serve immediately, or transfer to a slow cooker set to Warm until ready to serve.

2 Ladle the hot chocolate into mugs and top with whipped cream and marshmallows, if desired.

VARIATION To turn this into peppermint chocolate, add 2 Andes Mints to the bottom of your mug and stir with a candy cane. Divine! Creates the perfect holiday treat!

the cookie jar

♥

*A balanced diet is a cookie
in both hands!*

—BARBARA JOHNSON

The best cookies and bars to bring to a friend
or take to a party! Turn on the oven and grab your cutest apron.
With eleven of the best cookie recipes, you'll be whipping
up batches of cookies all year long!

────────────────── RECIPES ──────────────────

MAKES
36
cookies

- - - - - -

PREP
15 min

- - - - - -

CHILL
15 min

- - - - - -

COOK
8–10 min

- - - - - -

TOTAL
38–40 min

DOUBLE

chocolate chip sprinkle cookies

This cookie recipe is my go-to chocolate chip cookie with a fun addition of white chocolate chips and sprinkles. My daughter snuck in sprinkles one day when we were baking these cookies, and it's become a fun tradition for birthdays and celebrations. Sprinkles just make everything better, don't they? These cookies are super soft and chewy, with just the right amount of crispiness around the edges. They are absolutely perfect in my book!

♥

1 cup (2 sticks) unsalted butter, at room temperature

1 cup packed light brown sugar

¾ cup granulated sugar

2 large eggs

1 tablespoon vanilla extract

3 cups all-purpose flour

1 teaspoon baking soda

½ teaspoon cream of tartar

1 teaspoon salt

1½ cups milk or semisweet chocolate chips

½ cup white chocolate chips

¼ cup rainbow sprinkles

1 Preheat the oven to 350°F. Line two baking sheets with silicone baking mats or parchment paper.

2 In a large bowl, using a hand mixer, cream together the butter, brown sugar, and granulated sugar for 1 minute. Add the eggs and vanilla and mix until combined.

3 In a separate large bowl, whisk together the flour, baking soda, cream of tartar, and salt. Slowly add the flour mixture to the sugar mixture and mix until combined. Fold in the chocolate chips and sprinkles. Cover and refrigerate the dough for 15 minutes.

4 Using a medium cookie scoop (about 2 to 3 tablespoons), scoop the cookie dough onto the prepared baking sheets, spacing the portions at least 1 inch apart. Bake for 8 to 10 minutes, or until the edges are golden brown. They should still be soft and a little doughy in the middle. Remove from the oven and let the cookies cool on the baking sheets for 3 minutes, then transfer to a wire rack to cool completely.

5 Store in an airtight container at room temperature for up to 3 days.

i *heart* crafts

BIRTHDAY COOKIES

These are the sweetest treat to take to a friend on their birthday.
To dress them up, place the cookies in a clear bag and tie with ribbon and a tag.
You can also place them in a cute basket or metal tin. Photocopy a tag
from page 251, or download a printable version from my website at
www.iheartnaptime.net/book-template.

MAKES
24–36
cookies

PREP
25 min

CHILL
15–20 min

COOK
10–12 min

TOTAL
approx 55 min

CHOCOLATE

caramel crinkle cookies

Double chocolate cookies filled with chocolate chips and gooey caramel. These are so rich and decadent, and are sure to please any and all chocolate lovers. Grab a big glass of cold milk and dig in.

♥

1 cup (2 sticks) unsalted butter, at room temperature

2 cups granulated sugar

2 large eggs

2½ teaspoons vanilla extract

2 cups all-purpose flour

¾ cup unsweetened cocoa powder

1½ teaspoons baking soda

1½ teaspoons baking powder

1 teaspoon fine sea salt

½ cup semisweet chocolate chips

24–36 Rolo candies

¼ cup powdered or granulated sugar

HELPFUL · TIP ·

Invest in a silicone baking mat or parchment paper for lining pans. It will make cleanup a piece of cake and create softer baked goods.

1 Preheat the oven to 350°F. Line two baking sheets with parchment paper.

2 In a large bowl, using a hand mixer, cream together the butter and granulated sugar. Add the eggs and vanilla and mix until smooth.

3 In a separate large bowl, whisk together the flour, cocoa powder, baking soda, baking powder, and salt. Slowly pour the flour mixture into the sugar mixture and stir until well combined. Add the chocolate chips, then cover and refrigerate the dough for 15 to 20 minutes. (If you want these cooked more quickly, you can skip this step—the dough may be a little more sticky, so flour your hands before shaping the cookies.)

4 Shape the dough into 1½-inch balls. Press a Rolo into the center of each ball and cover the top with dough. Place the powdered sugar in a small bowl and roll each cookie in the sugar. Place the cookies on the prepared baking sheet as you work.

5 Bake for 10 to 12 minutes, or until the cookies are slightly crisp around the edges and soft in the middle. Let cool on the baking sheet for 2 minutes, then transfer to a wire rack.

6 Store in an airtight container at room temperature for up to 3 days.

sugar cookie bars
WITH CREAM CHEESE FROSTING

Nothing says the holidays quite like cookie-cutter sugar cookies decorated with cream cheese frosting. They are one of my favorites, but I tend to make them only around Christmas, since they take so much time. This recipe takes half the work of regular sugar cookies and the results are just as soft. It's very versatile, too: you can easily turn it into sugar cookies if you have more time (see the variations on page 192).

Use different food colorings and sprinkles to dress these up for any occasion. If you like a lot of frosting, simply double the recipe and have fun decorating.

MAKES
30
bars
- - - - - -
PREP
20 min
- - - - - -
COOK
15–17 min
- - - - - -
CHILL
20 min
- - - - - -
TOTAL
approx
1 hour

❤

1 **Make the cookies:** Preheat the oven to 350°F. Spray a jelly-roll pan (about 15 × 10 × 1 inch) with nonstick cooking spray. (Alternatively, you can use a 9 × 13-inch pan, which will result in slightly thicker bars.)

2 In a large bowl, using a hand mixer, beat together the butter and granulated sugar until fluffy. Add the egg, vanilla, and sour cream and mix until combined.

3 In a medium bowl, whisk together the flour, baking powder, baking soda, and salt. Slowly add the flour mixture to the sugar mixture and mix until combined.

4 Lightly flour your hands and press the dough evenly into the pan with your palms.

5 Bake for 15 to 17 minutes, or until a toothpick inserted into the center comes out clean. Do not let the top brown. Set on a wire rack and let cool completely.

6 **Make the cream cheese frosting:** In a medium bowl, using a hand mixer, beat together the butter and cream cheese until fluffy. Slowly add the powdered sugar, using more or less to suit your taste, the vanilla, and the salt. Mix until smooth and creamy. Frost the cooled sugar cookie bars.

For the cookies

Nonstick cooking spray

½ cup (1 stick) unsalted butter, at room temperature

1 cup granulated sugar

1 large egg

1½ teaspoons vanilla extract

½ cup sour cream

2¼ cups all-purpose flour, plus more for dusting

1 teaspoon baking powder

½ teaspoon baking soda

½ teaspoon salt

For the cream cheese frosting

4 tablespoons (½ stick) unsalted butter, at room temperature

½ (8-ounce) package cream cheese, at room temperature

1½ to 2 cups powdered sugar

1 teaspoon vanilla extract

Pinch of salt

recipe
CONTINUES

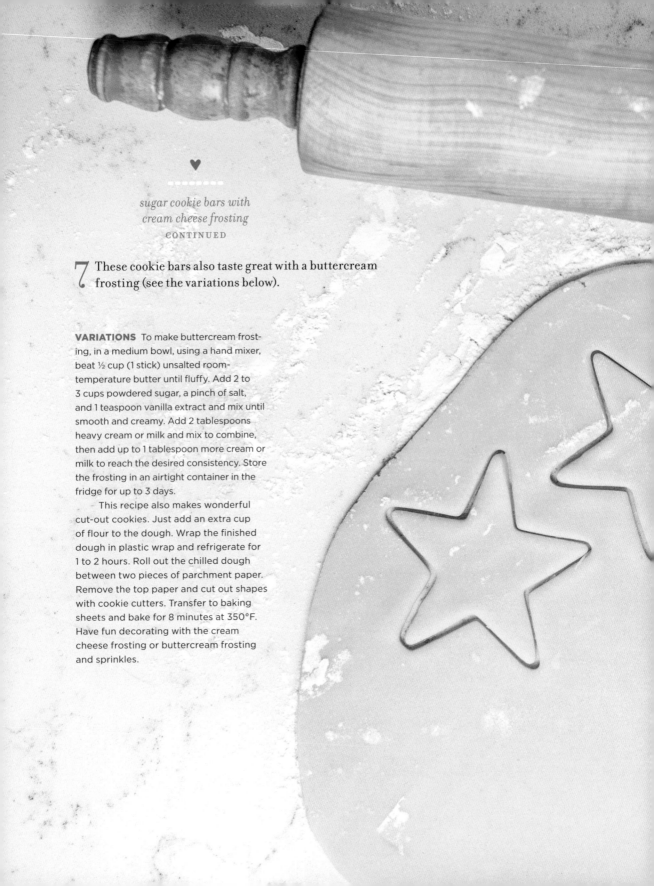

♥

- - - - - - - -

sugar cookie bars with
cream cheese frosting
CONTINUED

7 These cookie bars also taste great with a buttercream
frosting (see the variations below).

VARIATIONS To make buttercream frosting, in a medium bowl, using a hand mixer, beat ½ cup (1 stick) unsalted room-temperature butter until fluffy. Add 2 to 3 cups powdered sugar, a pinch of salt, and 1 teaspoon vanilla extract and mix until smooth and creamy. Add 2 tablespoons heavy cream or milk and mix to combine, then add up to 1 tablespoon more cream or milk to reach the desired consistency. Store the frosting in an airtight container in the fridge for up to 3 days.

This recipe also makes wonderful cut-out cookies. Just add an extra cup of flour to the dough. Wrap the finished dough in plastic wrap and refrigerate for 1 to 2 hours. Roll out the chilled dough between two pieces of parchment paper. Remove the top paper and cut out shapes with cookie cutters. Transfer to baking sheets and bake for 8 minutes at 350°F. Have fun decorating with the cream cheese frosting or buttercream frosting and sprinkles.

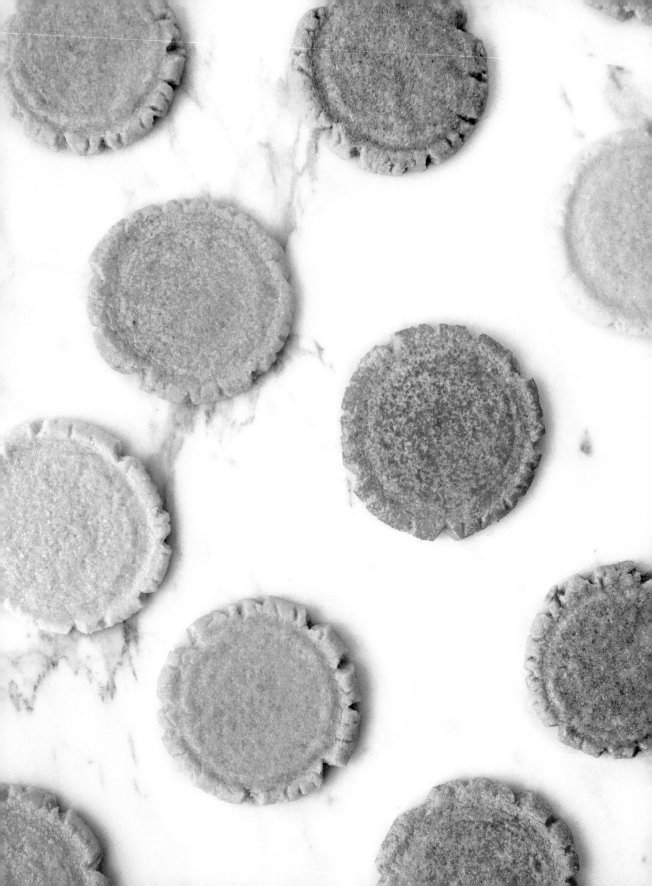

rainbow cookies

MAKES
24–36
cookies

PREP
20 min

COOK
8–10 min

TOTAL
28–30 min

These are colorful rainbow sugar cookies that the kids can help make and will absolutely adore. This recipe has been tweaked from one I shared on my blog a few years back. It went viral and was shared across social media channels more than a million times. I couldn't believe it!

I prefer these cookies plain, without the Jell-O, and I like to roll the dough in granulated sugar before baking, so I usually split the dough in half and bake some that way, too.

♥

1 Preheat the oven to 350°F. Line two baking sheets with silicone baking mats or parchment paper.

2 In a large bowl, using a hand mixer, beat together the butter, 3/4 cup of the granulated sugar, and the powdered sugar until fluffy. Add the oil, vanilla, and egg and mix for about 1 minute.

3 In a medium bowl, whisk together the flour, baking powder, salt, and cream of tartar. Slowly add the flour mixture to the sugar mixture and stir until combined.

4 Divide the dough in half. Sprinkle 2 tablespoons of the Jell-O mix on top of one half and then knead the dough until combined. You can add a few drops of food coloring at this point if you'd like the color to be more vibrant.

5 Place the remaining Jell-O mix in a small bowl. Roll the Jell-O dough into 1-inch balls and then roll them in the Jell-O mix. Place the remaining ¼ cup granulated sugar in a second bowl. Roll the plain dough into 1-inch balls and then roll in the granulated sugar. As you work, place the coated dough balls on the prepared baking sheet and gently press down on each with the bottom of a glass to flatten into a circle.

6 Bake for 8 to 10 minutes. Let cool on the baking sheets for a few minutes and then transfer to a wire rack.

7 Store in an airtight container at room temperature for up to 3 days.

½ cup (1 stick) unsalted butter

1 cup granulated sugar

⅓ cup powdered sugar

⅓ cup vegetable oil

1 teaspoon vanilla extract

1 large egg

2¼ cups all-purpose flour

1 teaspoon baking powder

½ teaspoon salt

¼ teaspoon cream of tartar

1 (3-ounce) package Jell-O mix (I like raspberry flavor best)

Food coloring (optional)

GET THE KIDS INVOLVED! Separate the dough into individual bowls and add a different food coloring to each. Let your kids mix up different colors using their hands (after they've been washed, of course). This is a fun activity for rainy days. You can even let them roll out the dough and cut it into shapes.

MAKES
24—36
cookies

- - - - - -

PREP
25 min

- - - - - -

COOK
8—11 min

- - - - - -

TOTAL
33—36 min

BOYFRIEND

cookies

Growing up I called these the boyfriend cookies, since I used to make them in college for all the boys I had a crush on. Luckily, they ended up winning my husband over. Imagine a big fat chewy cookie filled with loads of chocolate and crushed oatmeal. These cookies taste best warm out of the oven with a glass of cold milk.

♥

1 cup (2 sticks) unsalted butter

1 cup granulated sugar

1 cup packed light brown sugar

2 large eggs

2 teaspoons vanilla extract

2 cups all-purpose flour

1 teaspoon salt

1 teaspoon baking soda

1 teaspoon baking powder

1¼ cups old-fashioned rolled oats

1 (3- to 4-ounce) bar milk chocolate, frozen

1½ cups semisweet chocolate chips

¾ cup chocolate candies (I prefer M&M's)

½ cup walnuts, finely chopped (optional)

HELPFUL
·TIP·

If you don't have a chocolate bar, you can grind up ½ cup chocolate chips. You can also use the blender or food processor to chop the walnuts—just don't process them so much that they become a paste.

1 Preheat the oven to 350°F. Line two baking sheets with silicone baking mats or parchment paper.

2 In a large bowl, using a hand mixer, cream together the butter, granulated sugar, and brown sugar. Add the eggs and vanilla and mix until just combined.

3 In a large bowl, whisk together the flour, salt, baking soda, and baking powder. Place the oats in a blender and grind until fine. It's okay to have some chunks. Whisk the oats into the flour mixture and then slowly stir the flour mixture into the sugar mixture.

4 Place the frozen chocolate bar in the blender or food processor, and pulse about 5 to 10 times to grind it. Stir the chocolate flakes, chocolate chips, and chocolate candies into the dough. If desired, add the walnuts and stir until just combined.

5 Using a medium cookie scoop (about 2 to 3 tablespoons), scoop the cookie dough portions onto the prepared baking sheet at least 1 inch apart. Bake for 8 to 11 minutes, or until the edges are lightly golden brown. They should look a little doughy in the middle. Let the cookies cool on the baking sheets for a few minutes and then transfer to a wire rack. Store in an airtight container at room temperature for up to 3 days.

MAKES
24–30
cookies

PREP
25 min

COOK
10–12 min

TOTAL
35–37 min

SOFT CARAMEL

snickerdoodles

Say hello to soft and fluffy snickerdoodles stuffed with caramels. These cookies will soon become a new staple. They are a fun twist on the classic snickerdoodle everyone loves. These can also be made without caramel for a more traditional snickerdoodle, if you'd like.

♥

1 Preheat the oven to 350°F. Line two baking sheets with parchment paper.

2 In a large bowl, using a hand mixer, cream together the butter, 1 cup of the granulated sugar, and the brown sugar. Add the eggs and vanilla and beat until smooth.

3 In a separate large bowl, whisk together the flour, salt, baking powder, baking soda, and cream of tartar. Add the flour mixture to the butter mixture and stir until smooth. Cover the dough and refrigerate for 10 to 15 minutes.

4 In a small bowl, mix together the remaining ¼ cup granulated sugar and the cinnamon. Roll the dough into 1½-inch balls. Make an impression in the top of each cookie with your thumb and place 2 caramel pieces in each cookie. Pinch the top closed and roll the dough into a ball around the caramel. Roll the cookies in the cinnamon-sugar mixture and place on the prepared baking sheet about 1 inch apart.

5 Bake for 10 to 12 minutes, or until the edges are slightly crisp. You want the centers to still be soft. Let cool on the baking sheet for 3 minutes and then transfer to a wire rack.

6 Store in an airtight container at room temperature for up to 3 days.

1 cup (2 sticks) unsalted butter, at room temperature

1¼ cups granulated sugar

⅔ cup packed light brown sugar

2 large eggs

1½ teaspoons vanilla extract

3 cups all-purpose flour

½ teaspoon salt

1 teaspoon baking powder

1 teaspoon baking soda

1 teaspoon cream of tartar

1½ teaspoons ground cinnamon

12 soft caramels, cut into about ¼-inch pieces

HELPFUL
·TIP·

When baking, use the highest-quality ingredients you can. It really does make a difference in the taste.

MAKES
36
bars

- - - - - -

PREP
25 min

- - - - - -

COOK
20–25 min

- - - - - -

TOTAL
45–50 min

CHOCOLATE CHIP

s'mores bars

Ooey gooey s'mores bars…does it get any better than that?
The chewy center and marshmallows roasted on top are out of this world.
These are the perfect treat for a summer BBQ or to share with a friend!
My kids say these are the "best treat ever!"

Nonstick cooking spray (optional)

1 cup (2 sticks) unsalted butter, at room temperature

1 cup packed light brown sugar

¾ cup granulated sugar

2 large eggs

2 teaspoons vanilla extract

2 cups all-purpose flour, plus more for dusting

½ cup graham cracker crumbs

2 teaspoons baking powder

1 teaspoon table salt or fine sea salt

1 cup semisweet chocolate chips

1½ cups mini marshmallows

2 (1½-ounce) milk chocolate bars (I like to use Hershey's), broken into bite-size pieces

1 graham cracker, broken into bite-size pieces

1 Preheat the oven to 350°F. Line a 9 × 13-inch baking pan with aluminum foil or spray with nonstick cooking spray.

2 In a large bowl, using a hand mixer, cream together the butter, brown sugar, and granulated sugar. Add the eggs and vanilla and beat until combined.

3 In a separate medium bowl, whisk together the flour, graham cracker crumbs, baking powder, and salt. Slowly pour the flour mixture into the sugar mixture and stir until well combined. Stir in the chocolate chips and ¾ cup of the marshmallows.

4 Lightly flour your hands and transfer the dough to the prepared pan. Press the dough into the bottom of the pan. Gently sprinkle the chocolate bar pieces, graham cracker pieces, and the remaining ¾ cup marshmallows on top of the dough.

5 Bake for 20 to 25 minutes, or until the edges are lightly browned. The dough should still be soft in the center. Test with a toothpick to make sure it comes out clean. Let cool completely in the pan and then cut into 36 small squares. Enjoy with a glass of cold milk!

6 Store in an airtight container at room temperature for up to 3 days.

HELPFUL TIP

Before placing the fruit on the pizza, make sure any canned fruit has been drained and placed on a paper towel to remove excess moisture first, to avoid making the cookie soggy.

fruit pizza

I loved this dessert growing up. My mom used to make one for us on the Fourth of July and we always helped her decorate it like a flag. It is the ideal summertime treat to take to a BBQ. This fruit pizza is made with a soft sugar cookie crust, cream cheese filling, and fresh fruit topping. For a quicker crust, you can use one package of store-bought sugar cookie dough.

SERVES
12–16

PREP
20 min

COOK
18–22 min

CHILL
15 min

TOTAL
approx
1 hour

♥

1 **Make the sugar cookie crust:** Preheat the oven to 350°F. Spray a circular glass pizza dish or a jelly-roll pan (about 15 × 10 × 1 inch) with nonstick cooking spray.

2 In a large bowl, using a hand mixer, beat together the butter and sugar until fluffy. Add the egg, vanilla, and sour cream and mix until combined.

3 In a medium bowl, whisk together the flour, cream of tartar, baking soda, and salt. Slowly add the flour mixture to the sugar mixture and stir until combined.

4 Lightly flour your hands (or use a piece of waxed paper) and transfer the dough to the prepared baking dish. Press the dough evenly into the dish.

5 Bake for 18 to 22 minutes, or until a toothpick inserted into the center comes out clean. Do not let the top brown. Let cool, then freeze for 15 minutes to cool completely, if needed.

6 **Make the cream cheese frosting:** In a medium bowl, using a hand mixer, beat together the cream cheese, sugar, and vanilla. Mix in the nondairy whipped topping and stir until smooth. Spread the frosting evenly over the cooled sugar cookie crust.

7 Top the frosting with your favorite fruits in unique designs. My favorite fruits to add are strawberries, raspberries, mandarin oranges, and kiwi.

For the sugar cookie crust

Nonstick cooking spray

½ cup (1 stick) unsalted butter, at room temperature

1 cup sugar

1 large egg

2 teaspoons vanilla extract

½ cup sour cream

1¾ to 2 cups all-purpose flour, plus more for dusting

1 teaspoon cream of tartar

½ teaspoon baking soda

½ teaspoon salt

For the cream cheese frosting

1 (8-ounce) package cream cheese, at room temperature

¼ cup sugar

1½ teaspoons vanilla extract

3 cups frozen nondairy whipped topping, at room temperature

Optional fruit toppings: strawberries, raspberries, blueberries, pineapple, mandarin oranges, kiwi, grapes, bananas, peaches, and cherry pie filling

MAKES
36
cookies

PREP
15 min

CHILL
15 min

COOK
10–12 min

TOTAL
approx
45 min

WHITE CHOCOLATE
cranberry
macadamia nut cookies

These cookies are irresistible and loaded with white chocolate, dried cranberries, and macadamia nuts. They are super soft, chewy, and crispy around the edges. Whip up a batch of these on a lazy Sunday afternoon, for a cookie exchange, or for a holiday party.

1 cup (2 sticks) unsalted butter, at room temperature

1 cup packed light brown sugar

¾ cup granulated sugar

2 large eggs

2 teaspoons vanilla extract

2¾ cups all-purpose flour

1 teaspoon table salt or fine sea salt

1 teaspoon baking powder

1 cup white chocolate chips or chunks

¾ cup dried cranberries

½ cup chopped macadamia nuts

1 Preheat the oven to 350°F. Line two baking sheets with silicone baking mats or parchment paper.

2 In a large bowl, using a hand mixer, cream together the butter, brown sugar, and granulated sugar. Add the eggs and vanilla and mix until combined.

3 In a medium bowl, whisk together the flour, salt, and baking powder. Slowly add the flour mixture to the sugar mixture and stir until combined. Fold in the chocolate chips, cranberries, and macadamia nuts. Cover and refrigerate the dough for 15 minutes.

4 Using a medium cookie scoop (about 2 to 3 tablespoons), scoop the cookie dough portions onto the prepared baking sheet at least 1 inch apart. Bake for 10 to 12 minutes, or until the edges are golden brown. The cookies should still be soft and a little doughy in the middle. Let cool on the baking sheet for 3 minutes and then transfer to a wire rack.

5 Store in an airtight container at room temperature for up to 3 days.

brownie ice cream sandwiches

*Gooey chocolate brownie cookies stuffed with peanut butter and ice cream?
Yup, I went there! Roll these ice cream sandwiches with your favorite toppings
or dip one side into chocolate for an extra-special treat. These couldn't be
easier to make and are the best summer indulgence!*

MAKES
8
ice cream
sandwiches

PREP
15 min

COOK
8 min

CHILL
25 min

TOTAL
approx
50 min

♥

1 Preheat the oven to 375°F. Line a baking sheet with a silicone baking mat or parchment paper.

2 In a medium bowl, beat together the brownie mix, eggs, and vegetable oil for 2 minutes, or until smooth. Stir in the chocolate chips (if using).

3 Using a medium cookie scoop (about 2 to 3 tablespoons), scoop the cookie dough portion onto the prepared baking sheet, at least 1 inch apart. Bake for 10 to 12 minutes, or until the edges are golden brown. They should still be soft and a little doughy in the middle. Let cool on the baking sheet for 3 minutes and then transfer to a wire rack.

4 Once completely cool, spread 1 tablespoon of the peanut butter onto the flat side of half of the cookies. Then, using an ice cream scoop, add one scoop of ice cream. Top with a second cookie and press down slightly. Place the sandwiches on a baking sheet and freeze for 20 minutes, or until set.

5 Make the chocolate shell (optional): In a small microwave-safe bowl, combine the chocolate and oil. Microwave for 1 to 2 minutes at 50% power. Stir and microwave for 1 minute more, or until melted.

1 (about 18-ounce) box brownie mix

2 large eggs

⅓ cup vegetable oil

½ cup mini chocolate chips (optional)

½ cup smooth peanut butter

½ pint vanilla ice cream, slightly softened

For the chocolate shell (optional)

8 ounces semisweet chocolate, chopped

2 teaspoons vegetable oil or coconut oil

recipe
CONTINUES

peanut butter brownie
ice cream sandwiches
CONTINUED

Line your baking sheets and pans with parchment paper or aluminum foil before making brownies or bars. When they are done cooking, you can easily pull out the paper or foil and cut the bars. It also makes cleanup a breeze.

6 Dip one side of each chilled ice cream sandwich into the chocolate shell and return to the freezer for 5 minutes, or until set.

7 Wrap the ice cream sandwiches individually in parchment paper or aluminum foil and store in the freezer for up to 1 month.

NOTE *Once frozen, you may cut these in half with a sharp knife for smaller portions and then wrap them.*

VARIATION Try using mint or white chocolate chips. You may also omit the peanut butter and try different fillings such as Dreamy Caramel Sauce (page 242).

MAKES
36
cookies

PREP
20 min

COOK
10 min

CHILL
15 min

TOTAL
45 min

pumpkin cookies

When we moved to Ohio for my husband's residency, I quickly fell in love with autumn. With fall comes the leaves changing, pumpkin patches, apple cider, and, of course, pumpkin desserts.

Whenever I take these pumpkin cookies to a get-together, my friends always ask for the recipe. They are the perfect cookie to celebrate autumn, although we love making them year-round, too. These pumpkin cookies are so soft and the caramel frosting is worth making all on its own. These do take a few extra dishes, but I promise, they will be worth it.

♥

For the cookies

1 cup (2 sticks) unsalted butter, at room temperature

⅔ cup packed light brown sugar

⅓ cup granulated sugar

1 large egg

1½ teaspoons vanilla extract

1 cup pumpkin puree (not pumpkin pie mix)

2 cups all-purpose flour

1 teaspoon baking soda

2 teaspoons pumpkin pie spice

1½ teaspoons ground cinnamon

¾ teaspoon table salt

For the caramel frosting

4 tablespoons (½ stick) unsalted butter

3 tablespoons heavy cream, plus more as needed

½ cup packed light brown sugar

Pinch of salt

1½ teaspoons vanilla extract

1 cup powdered sugar, sifted

1 **Make the cookies:** Preheat the oven to 350°F. Line two baking sheets with silicone baking mats or parchment paper.

2 In a large bowl, using a hand mixer, cream together the butter, brown sugar, and granulated sugar. Add the egg and vanilla and beat until combined. Add the pumpkin and mix until smooth.

3 In a separate large bowl, whisk together the flour, baking soda, pumpkin pie spice, cinnamon, and salt. Slowly add to the wet pumpkin mixture and beat until just combined.

4 Using a medium cookie scoop or large spoon, scoop the cookie dough onto the prepared baking sheet, spacing the portions two inches apart. Bake for 10 minutes, or until a toothpick inserted into the center of a cookie comes out clean. Let cool on the baking sheet for 2 minutes, then transfer to a wire rack to cool completely.

5 **Make the caramel frosting:** In a small saucepan, combine the butter, heavy cream, brown sugar, and salt and, while whisking, bring to a boil over medium heat. Boil for 1 to 2 minutes. Pour the caramel mixture into a medium bowl and let cool for 1 minute.

6 Add the vanilla and powdered sugar and stir until smooth. Frost the cookies immediately with a rubber spatula, as the frosting will begin to firm up quickly.

7 Store in an airtight container or large zip-top bags at room temperature or in the refrigerator for up to 1 week.

VARIATIONS These pumpkin cookies also taste great with cream cheese frosting (see page 237). You can also stir 1 cup chocolate chips into the dough before baking and then forgo the frosting.

CHAPTER 1

sweet treats

♥

Life is short. Eat dessert first.

—JACQUES TORRES

Have a sweet tooth? Then this chapter's for you.
This collection of desserts and sweet treats is sure to please.
You won't be able to choose just one to make! In our house,
Sundays are for baking, and these are a few of our favorite recipes
to make when we're craving something sweet.

RECIPES

MAKES
ABOUT
15 CUPS,
to serve
12–15

- - - - - -

PREP
10 min

- - - - - -

COOK
10 min

- - - - - -

TOTAL
20 min

MARSHMALLOW

caramel popcorn

I have never met anyone who doesn't adore this recipe. This popcorn is one that is always requested by friends and family. It is super soft, sticky, delicious, and easy to make. The marshmallow mixture reminds me of my favorite Rice Krispies treats, but the brown sugar takes it to a whole new level! It travels well, making it a great dessert to take to a party.

♥

15 cups popped lightly salted popcorn (about 2 bags microwave popcorn)

1 cup (2 sticks) unsalted butter

8 cups mini marshmallows (about one 16-ounce bag)

¾ cup packed light brown sugar

½ teaspoon vanilla extract

½ teaspoon table salt or fine sea salt

½ cup candy-coated chocolate candies (optional)

¼ to ½ cup semisweet chocolate chips (optional)

1 Place a 24-inch piece of waxed paper on the counter. Put the popcorn in a large bowl and pick out any unpopped kernels. Set aside.

2 In a large saucepan, melt the butter and marshmallows over medium-low heat. Once the butter has melted, stir in the brown sugar and cook for about 2 minutes, or until it has dissolved. Remove from the heat and stir in the vanilla and salt. Pour the marshmallow-caramel mixture over the popcorn and carefully stir (it will be hot!) until completely coated. Pour the popcorn out onto the waxed paper sheet and sprinkle with the chocolate candies, if desired.

3 If desired, place the chocolate chips in a microwave-safe bowl and melt in the microwave for about 1 minute, or until smooth. Drizzle the chocolate over the popcorn with a spoon. Let cool to room temperature before serving.

4 Store in an airtight container or zip-top bag at room temperature. It is best served fresh, or within 2 to 3 days.

HELPFUL
·TIP·

Measure your salt over a separate bowl, so that you don't accidentally pour too much salt into your mixing bowl. I had to learn that one the hard way!

MAKES
16–20
tarts

- - - - - - -

PREP
15 min

- - - - - - -

COOL
15 min

- - - - - - -

TOTAL
30 min

MINI NO-BAKE

cheesecake tarts

These bite-size, no-bake cheesecakes are an easy and delightful summer treat. The filling is rich, yet fresh and much creamier than your traditional cheesecake. The tarts can be customized with your favorite toppings and whipped up in no time. These cheesecakes can also easily be made with my no-bake graham cracker crust, or you can use premade tart shells to speed things up.

♥

For the cream cheese filling

1 (8-ounce) package cream cheese

1½ tablespoons granulated sugar

1 teaspoon vanilla extract

½ cup sweetened condensed milk

1 tablespoon fresh lemon juice (optional)

1 package of 16 premade mini tart shells (optional)

For the graham cracker crust (optional)

1½ cups graham cracker crumbs

2 tablespoons brown sugar

½ cup (1 stick) unsalted butter, melted

For the strawberry topping (optional)

1 cup finely chopped strawberries

1½ tablespoons granulated sugar

Optional toppings: fresh raspberries, fresh blueberries, cherry pie filling, Dreamy Caramel Sauce (page 242), Homemade Hot Fudge (page 249), chopped nuts

1 **Make the cream cheese filling:** In a medium bowl, using a hand mixer, beat together the cream cheese, granulated sugar, and vanilla until creamy. Add the condensed milk and lemon juice (if using) and mix until just combined. If using the tart shells, spoon the filling into the shells.

2 **Make the graham cracker crust (optional):** If you prefer to make the graham cracker crust, in a small bowl, using a fork, combine the graham cracker crumbs, brown sugar, and butter. Press the mixture firmly into the bottom of a 9-inch pie pan or individual 4-ounce mason jars or cups and add the filling.

3 Freeze the tarts for 15 minutes, then store in the refrigerator until ready to serve.

4 **Make the strawberry topping (optional):** Combine the strawberries and sugar in a small bowl. Stir until the strawberries are well coated and then refrigerate for 30 minutes.

5 Add your favorite toppings, such as the strawberry topping, to the tarts just before serving.

A CAKE FOR YOU

To turn these into a gift, make the cheesecakes in 4-ounce mason jars and tie ribbon or twine around the top of the jars with gift tags. You could also tie on a wooden spoon to make for easy snacking. Another fun way to decorate the jar is to cut a square piece of fabric and secure it around the top with twine.

chocolate mug cake

This quick-and-easy chocolate mug cake will change your life. It is super rich, soft, delicious, and done in five minutes, with little cleanup! It's perfect for those emergency chocolate cravings…you know the ones. I had many late-night chocolate cravings during my last pregnancy. It also makes a great dessert for a date night at home when all you want to do is watch a movie on the couch. Get creative and add your favorite ice cream sundae toppings, like Dreamy Caramel Sauce (page 242) or Homemade Hot Fudge (page 249).

MAKES
1
cake

PREP
4 min

COOK
1 min

TOTAL
5 min

¼ cup low-fat milk

2½ tablespoons salted butter, cut into small pieces

3½ tablespoons granulated sugar

½ scant teaspoon vanilla extract

¼ cup all-purpose flour

¼ teaspoon baking powder

2 tablespoons unsweetened cocoa powder

1 to 2 tablespoons mini chocolate chips

Ice cream or whipped cream (optional)

Sundae toppings (optional)

1 Place the milk and butter in a 14-ounce glass mug or small microwavable bowl. Microwave for 30 seconds, or until the butter has melted.

2 Add the sugar and vanilla and stir until the sugar has begun to dissolve. Add the flour, baking powder, and cocoa powder and mix with a fork until smooth. Stir in the chocolate chips and then microwave on high for 60 seconds, or until a toothpick inserted into the center comes out clean.

3 Enjoy plain, or topped with a scoop of ice cream or whipped cream and your favorite sundae toppings.

HELPFUL TIP

Since all microwaves cook differently, you may need to cook for an additional 10 to 15 seconds if the middle is not cooked all the way through. Also, if making more than one mug cake, microwave them separately.

Learn how to create your own personalized mug on page 220. Give it as a gift using a gift tag from the template on page 254.

Mug Cake

- - - - - - - - - - - -

1/4 c. milk	1/4 c. flour
2 1/4 T. butter	1/4 t. baking p.
3 1/2 T. sugar	2 T cocoa.
1/2 t. vanilla	2 T choc. chips

Microwave 60 sec.

Add ice cream

i *heart* crafts

DIY MUG OR PLATE

PROJECT TIME: 45 MIN

Glass or ceramic mug or plate (I
   like to buy mine at thrift stores
   or boutiques)

Black fine-point permanent
   marker

1 Draw a design onto the mug or plate with your permanent
marker. Preheat the oven to 450°F and place the mug or plate
in the oven for 30 minutes. Turn off the oven and let the mug or
plate cool for 10 minutes inside the oven, then remove from the
oven to finish cooling.

2 Hand-wash only.

**HELPFUL
TIP**

My kids love
decorating mugs
for their teachers
and grandparents.
You can fill
them with treats.

A BASKET OF TOFFEE

For a fun way to package the toffee on page 222, place a piece of parchment paper inside a berry basket and then fill with toffee. You can also package it in a jar or metal tin tied with twine or ribbon.

SERVES
15–20

PREP
10 min

COOK
7–8 min

CHILL
15 min

TOTAL
32–33 min

SALTINE CRACKER

toffee

While this recipe is different from your traditional toffee, it is seriously addictive and it's much easier! It takes sweet *and* salty *to a whole new level. This recipe comes from my Gramma and is a family favorite that we make every holiday. It tastes great plain, without chocolate, but is even better dressed up with chocolate and sliced almonds. We usually like to do half the batch plain and half with chocolate to get the best of both worlds.*

♥

Nonstick cooking spray

About 50 saltine crackers

1 cup (2 sticks) salted butter, cut into cubes

1 cup packed light brown sugar

1 cup semisweet or milk chocolate chips (optional)

¼ cup sliced almonds, chopped pecans, toffee bits, or M&M's (optional)

1 Preheat the oven to 325°F. Line a large rimmed baking sheet (18 × 13 inches) or jelly-roll pan with aluminum foil. Spray the foil with nonstick cooking spray. Arrange the crackers in a single layer over the foil.

2 In a medium saucepan, combine the butter and brown sugar and cook over medium-low heat, stirring, until the butter has melted and the sugar has dissolved. Bring the mixture to a boil over medium heat and cook, stirring continuously, for 3 minutes. Once it's bubbling and the butter and sugar have combined, remove the pan from the heat and pour the mixture evenly over the crackers. Try to move fast during this part so the toffee doesn't harden.

3 Bake for 7 to 8 minutes, or until golden brown. The toffee will spread evenly over the crackers as it bakes. Remove the pan from the oven. Melt the chocolate chips (if using) in a microwave-safe bowl for 1 minute or until melted. Then spread them all over the toffee-covered crackers with a rubber or offset spatula. Sprinkle nuts, toffee bits, or M&M's on top, if desired, and then press down lightly with the spatula. Freeze for 15 minutes, or until the chocolate has hardened. Break pieces off the foil and store in an airtight container at room temperature for up to 2 weeks.

VARIATION You can also make this toffee with graham, Ritz, or club crackers.

CHOCOLATE

peanut butter truffles

Chocolate and peanut butter were made for each other, don't you think? These peanut butter truffles are so easy to make and are the perfect treat for a party. This is a great no-bake recipe that the kids can help with. They almost taste like a homemade peanut butter cup, but even better! This recipe can easily be doubled for a large crowd, and are adorable served in mini cupcake liners.

MAKES
ABOUT 20
truffles

PREP
20 min

COOL
30 min

TOTAL
50 min

1 Line a baking sheet with waxed paper.

2 In a medium bowl, using a hand mixer, beat together the peanut butter, butter, and vanilla. Gradually sift in 1 cup of the powdered sugar and mix until well combined. Add the remaining ½ cup powdered sugar and mix with your hands until all the sugar is combined.

3 Shape the dough into 1-inch balls and place them on the prepared baking sheet. I like to use a small cookie scoop or a tablespoon measure. Freeze the truffles for 15 minutes.

4 In a small microwave-safe bowl, combine the chocolate chips and shortening and melt in the microwave for 60 to 80 seconds. (Alternatively, melt the chocolate and shortening together in the top of a double boiler.) If using the candy melts or wafers, you will not need the shortening. Stir until melted and well combined.

5 Dip the truffles one by one into the melted chocolate. Make sure they are evenly and completely coated. I use a fork to dip them, and then tap the fork on the side of the bowl to remove any excess chocolate. Place the chocolate-coated truffles back on the lined baking sheet. Top with a bit of sea salt, if desired. Return the truffles to the freezer for at least 15 minutes to harden the chocolate. Store the truffles in an airtight container in the refrigerator up to 1 week.

VARIATION You can also roll them in crushed nuts, mini chocolate chips, powdered sugar, coconut, or sprinkles instead.

¾ cup creamy peanut butter

4 tablespoons (½ stick) unsalted butter, at room temperature

½ teaspoon vanilla extract

1½ cups powdered sugar, sifted

2 cups semisweet chocolate chips or chocolate candy melts

1 tablespoon shortening (optional)

Flaky sea salt (optional)

HELPFUL · TIP ·

One of the easiest ways to melt chocolate is in the microwave. Place your chocolate in a microwave-safe bowl and microwave at 50% power for 1 minute. Let sit in the microwave for 30 seconds, then remove the bowl and stir. If the chocolate is not completely melted, microwave again at 50% power for 15 seconds and stir until smooth.

TRUFFLES TO GO

Place the truffles inside mini cupcake liners. Then fill a cupcake box with shredded filler and set the truffles inside. Tie with a ribbon or twine. Another fun way to deliver these treats is to wrap them individually in waxed or tissue paper and tie the ends with ribbon.

Enjoy a sweet!

brownie bites

I adore the combination of chocolate and mint. They go together perfectly. These chocolate mint brownie bites are just right for the holidays, baby showers, or anytime, really. I love to use a brownie mix with these to make them quickly, and they really do come together in no time!

MAKES
36
brownie bites

PREP
15 min

COOK
15 min

COOL
15 min

TOTAL
45 min

♥

1 **Make the brownie bites:** Preheat the oven to 325°F. Line a mini-muffin pan with paper liners and spray the liners with nonstick cooking spray.

2 In a medium bowl, mix together the brownie mix, butter, buttermilk, vanilla, and egg.

3 Fold in the chocolate chips and mix until combined. Pour the batter into the liners, filling them two-thirds of the way. The brownies will rise while baking. Bake for 10 to 15 minutes, or until a toothpick inserted into the center comes out clean. Let cool for a few minutes in the pan and then transfer to a wire rack to cool completely.

4 **Make the mint frosting:** In a medium bowl, using a hand mixer, beat the butter until fluffy. Slowly add the powdered sugar, cream, and peppermint extract and mix until smooth. Add more cream, 1 teaspoon at a time, if necessary, to reach the desired consistency. You want the frosting to be stiff but spreadable. Add green food coloring, if desired.

5 Transfer the frosting to a piping bag fitted with a large round tip (or use a zip-top bag with one corner snipped off) and frost the cupcakes. (Alternatively, you can spread the frosting on with a spatula.) Place 1 mint piece on top of each brownie cup and serve. Store in a covered container for up to 3 days, or place in the freezer.

For the brownie bites

Nonstick cooking spray

1 (about 18-ounce) box brownie mix

6 tablespoons salted butter, melted

¼ cup buttermilk

1½ teaspoons vanilla extract

1 large egg

½ cup mini chocolate chips

For the mint frosting

4 tablespoons (½ stick) unsalted butter, at room temperature

2 cups powdered sugar

2 tablespoons heavy cream, plus more as needed

½ teaspoon peppermint extract

Green food coloring (optional)

18 Andes Mints, broken into 2 pieces each

VARIATION For thick, chewy, fudgy brownies, pour the batter into a lined 8 x 8-inch baking pan and cook for 35 to 40 minutes, or until a toothpick comes out clean. Then top with half a batch of the chocolate icing on page 238. Yum!

SERVES
12–15

PREP
10 min

COOK
10 min

TOTAL
20 min

HEAVENLY

chex mix

Ooey gooey Chex mix topped with fresh coconut, sliced almonds, and a caramel coating: this is Chex mix at its finest. This heavenly snack is seriously addictive, and it's been made in our family for years. The pretzels add a nice salty touch. Just one bite and you'll be hooked!

Nonstick cooking spray

8 cups Rice Chex cereal

1 to 2 cups sweetened coconut flakes

½ cup sliced almonds, plus more if desired

1 cup salted pretzel sticks, broken into 1-inch pieces (optional)

¾ cup (1½ sticks) salted butter, cut into cubes

1 cup sugar

1 cup light corn syrup

1 teaspoon vanilla extract

1 cup mini marshmallows (optional)

1 Spray a large bowl with nonstick cooking spray. Pour the Chex cereal into the bowl and mix in the coconut, nuts, and pretzels (if using). Set aside.

2 In a large saucepan, combine the butter, sugar, and corn syrup and heat over medium heat, stirring, until the butter has melted. Raise the heat to medium-high. Bring to a boil and cook, stirring continuously, for 3 minutes, or until the sugar has dissolved. Remove the pan from the heat and add the vanilla. Stir until combined.

3 Carefully pour the mixture over the Chex mix and stir until the cereal is coated. Stir in the marshmallows (if using), and then spread the mixture onto a baking sheet lined with waxed paper and let cool. Store in an airtight container at room temperature for up to 1 week.

VARIATION Use a different mix of nuts, such as cashews or pecans.

apple doughnuts

These apple doughnuts are a fun and healthy treat, and the kids will love to roll up their sleeves and decorate them with you. They remind me of a gourmet caramel apple, but are much easier to make. Dress up the apples with toppings such as coconut, sprinkles, chocolate chips, nuts, and Dreamy Caramel Sauce (page 242).

MAKES
12
apple
doughnuts

PREP
10 min

TOTAL
10 min

1 Cut each apple crosswise into ¼-inch-thick slices. Core the slices with a knife or using a 1-inch round cookie cutter. Place the apples on a baking sheet lined with waxed paper and drizzle melted chocolate (or sauce of your choice) and sprinkle your favorite toppings on top of the apple slices.

Here are a few of our favorite combinations:

- Chocolate with peanut butter and chocolate chips
- White chocolate, caramel, toasted coconut, and sliced almonds
- Marshmallow crème and sprinkles (the kids' favorite)

3 or 4 large tart apples

¼ cup chocolate chips, melted

OR

¼ cup smooth peanut butter, melted

Optional toppings: coconut flakes, sprinkles, chocolate chips, Craisins, nuts, granola, toffee bits, marshmallow crème, Homemade Hot Fudge (page 249), Dreamy Caramel Sauce (page 242)

MAKES
15–20
bars

- - - - - -

PREP
15 min

- - - - - -

COOK
30 min

- - - - - -

TOTAL
45 min

SEVEN-LAYER

chocolate pretzel bars

I always loved making seven-layer bars, also known as Hello Dollies, with my mom during the holidays. I've added a fun twist to the original recipe by adding a pretzel crust and chocolate ganache filling. These are very rich and absolutely heavenly, and they are perfect washed down with a tall glass of milk.

- ♥ -

1½ cups finely ground salted pretzels (4 to 5 cups whole pretzels)

¾ cup (1½ sticks) salted butter, melted, plus 2 tablespoons salted butter, cold

2 tablespoons sugar

¾ cup semisweet chocolate chips

1 (14-ounce) can sweetened condensed milk

⅔ cup chopped walnuts or pecans

1 cup sweetened coconut flakes

¼ cup white chocolate chips

¼ cup butterscotch chips (optional)

1 Preheat the oven to 400°F. Line a 9 × 13-inch baking pan with aluminum foil.

2 In a medium bowl, combine the pretzel crumbs, melted butter, and sugar and stir until combined. Press the pretzel crust firmly into the prepared pan and bake for 7 to 10 minutes, or until lightly browned.

3 Meanwhile, in a small saucepan, melt ½ cup of the chocolate chips and the remaining 2 tablespoons butter over medium-low heat. Stir in ⅓ cup of the condensed milk. Drizzle the chocolate sauce over the warm pretzel crust immediately and gently smooth it with a rubber spatula. Sprinkle the chopped walnuts over the top and drizzle with the remaining condensed milk. Finally, sprinkle the coconut, remaining ¼ cup chocolate chips, white chocolate chips, and butterscotch chips (if using) on top.

4 Bake for 15 minutes, or until the coconut is lightly browned. Keep a close eye on the bars while baking, as the condensed milk may brown. Lift the bars out of the pan using the foil and set on a wire rack to cool before cutting.

5 Once cooled, I like to cut the bars into small squares and serve them in mini cupcake wrappers.

VARIATION For a more traditional seven-layer bar, you may use graham cracker crumbs instead of pretzels.

banana bars

with CREAM CHEESE FROSTING

MAKES
28–35
bars

PREP
20 min

COOK
20–25 min

TOTAL
40–45 min

I'm always happy to have an excuse to make these delicious bars when we're stuck with overripe bananas. They are sweet, soft, and full of banana flavor. The cream cheese frosting truly takes these over the top.

♥

1 **Make the bars:** Preheat the oven to 350°F. Butter a large rimmed baking sheet.

2 In a large bowl, using a hand mixer, cream together the butter, granulated sugar, and brown sugar. Add the eggs, sour cream, and vanilla. Mix until well combined.

3 In a medium bowl, whisk together the flour, baking soda, baking powder, salt, and cinnamon. Slowly add the flour mixture to the sugar mixture and stir until smooth. Fold in the bananas (and walnuts, if desired) and mix until just combined.

4 Pour the mixture into the prepared pan and bake for 20 to 25 minutes, or until a toothpick inserted into the center comes out clean. Let the bars cool completely. You can place the pan in the freezer to speed up the process.

5 **Make the frosting:** While the bars are cooling, in a medium bowl, using a hand mixer, beat together the butter and cream cheese. Slowly add the powdered sugar, salt, and vanilla and mix until smooth and creamy.

6 Once the bars have cooled, use a rubber spatula to spread the frosting over them, then slice them into bars. Store in the refrigerator until ready to serve.

For the bars

½ cup (1 stick) unsalted butter, at room temperature, plus more for the pan

1 cup granulated sugar

½ cup packed light brown sugar

2 large eggs

1 cup sour cream

1½ teaspoons vanilla extract

2¼ cups all-purpose flour

1 teaspoon baking soda

½ teaspoon baking powder

½ teaspoon salt

½ teaspoon ground cinnamon

2 cups mashed ripe bananas (5 small bananas)

½ cup walnuts, chopped (optional)

For the frosting

½ cup (1 stick) unsalted butter

½ (8-ounce) package cream cheese

1½ to 2 cups powdered sugar

Pinch of salt

1½ teaspoons vanilla extract

SERVES
35

- - - - - -

PREP
20 min

- - - - - -

COOK
20 min

- - - - - -

TOTAL
40 min

CHOCOLATE
coconut sheet cake

This cake is perfectly sweet and full of chocolaty goodness. It reminds me of an Almond Joy, but with much more chocolate. The toasted coconut adds a nice touch to the traditional and beloved chocolate sheet cake. Not a huge fan of coconut? This cake can easily be made without it as well.

♥

For the toasted coconut

¾ cup sweetened coconut flakes

For the cake

Nonstick cooking spray

2 cups all-purpose flour

1 cup granulated sugar

1 cup packed light brown sugar

1 teaspoon baking soda

½ teaspoon table salt

1 cup (2 sticks) unsalted butter

1 cup milk

¼ cup unsweetened cocoa powder

½ cup sour cream

2 large eggs, whisked

1 tablespoon vanilla extract

¾ cup sweetened coconut flakes

For the icing

½ cup (1 stick) unsalted butter

3½ tablespoons unsweetened cocoa powder

⅓ cup milk

1 teaspoon vanilla extract

¼ teaspoon table salt or fine sea salt

3 cups powdered sugar, sifted

Dreamy Caramel Sauce (page 242), for topping (optional)

1 Make the toasted coconut: Preheat the oven to 350°F. Line a large (18 × 13-inch) rimmed baking sheet with aluminum foil and spread the coconut evenly over the pan. Toast in the oven for 7 to 10 minutes, or until golden brown. Stir the coconut halfway through to prevent the bottom from burning. Transfer to a plate to cool.

2 Make the cake: Grease the same baking sheet with nonstick cooking spray. In a large bowl, combine the flour, granulated sugar, brown sugar, baking soda, and salt. Set aside.

3 In a medium saucepan, melt the butter over low heat. Stir in the milk and cocoa powder. Bring to a light simmer and then remove from the heat and let cool slightly. Slowly add the butter mixture to the flour mixture and stir until combined. Stir in the sour cream, eggs, and vanilla. Add the coconut and stir just until combined. Pour the mixture into the prepared pan. Bake for 20 minutes, or until a toothpick inserted into the center comes out clean.

4 Make the icing: While the cake is baking, in a medium saucepan, melt the butter over low heat. Stir in the cocoa powder and bring the mixture to a light simmer. Remove from the heat and stir in the milk, vanilla, and salt. Slowly stir in the powdered sugar.

5 Immediately after the cake comes out of the oven, pour the icing evenly over the top. Immediately sprinkle the toasted coconut on top of the icing while it is still hot.

6 Let cool and then cut into squares. For an extra-special touch, drizzle caramel sauce on top.

GRAMMA'S

homemade caramels

MAKES
48
caramels
- - - - - -
PREP
10 min
- - - - - -
COOK
30 min
- - - - - -
CHILL
1 hour
- - - - - -
TOTAL
1 hour
40 min

I had to, *had to* include this recipe in my cookbook. This is one recipe that will take longer than one hour (since they have to harden), but it is worth the wait. Promise!

Growing up, we always visited my Gramma during Christmas break. After I gave her a big hug, I'd run right over to her dessert stash. She always had homemade caramels and divinity hidden in an old metal film tin. It was a real treat and a tradition I love to carry on during the holidays. These caramels are super soft and chewy, and you'll want to make them year after year.

♥

1 Butter a large piece of parchment paper and press it into a 9 × 13-inch baking dish.

2 In a large saucepan, combine the sugar, corn syrup, and salt over medium-high heat. Stir until the sugar has dissolved and the mixture has started to bubble. Slowly stir in the cream. Don't let it stop boiling, and keep stirring. Clip a candy thermometer to the side of the pan. Stir in the butter. Keep the mixture at a boil and stir continuously for about 15 minutes. When the temperature has reached 240°F (in between soft and firm ball stage), stir in the vanilla. Remove from the heat and pour into the prepared baking dish.

3 Let sit on the counter until firmed up, about 1 hour. Once the caramel has firmed up, lift it out of the pan using the parchment paper. Then use a buttered or plastic knife to cut it into 12 vertical rows and 4 horizontal rows, making a total of 48 caramel squares. Cut forty-eight 3 × 6-inch rectangles from waxed paper and wrap the caramels inside. The caramels will stay soft and chewy for up to 2 weeks.

½ cup (1 stick) salted butter, cut into cubes, plus more for the baking dish

2 cups sugar

2 cups light corn syrup

¼ teaspoon table salt or fine sea salt

2 cups heavy cream

1½ teaspoons vanilla extract

HELPFUL ·TIP·

Here's an easy way to test if the caramel is ready: Drop a teaspoon of caramel into a small glass of ice water. If the caramel forms a firm ball, it's ready. If it's still liquid and stringy, keep boiling and stirring. I like to use a candy thermometer as well to make sure it has reached at least 240°F.

MAKES
2 CUPS
- - - - - -
PREP
5 min
- - - - - -
COOK
15 min
- - - - - -
TOTAL
20 min

DREAMY

caramel sauce

This caramel sauce has been nicknamed "pure liquid gold" at my house.
It is dangerous stuff, I tell ya! It can be used for so many things, and tastes
amazing on top of vanilla ice cream, apple cider, pies, cakes, brownies,
apples, and more. If there was a swimming pool full of this caramel sauce, I
would dive right in! It is that good.

♥

1½ cups sugar

½ cup (1 stick) salted butter, cut into
cubes, at room temperature

¾ cup heavy cream, at room
temperature

¼ teaspoon fine sea salt

1 In a large saucepan, heat the sugar over medium heat,
stirring continuously with a whisk or spoon, for 5 to
7 minutes. The sugar will begin to turn clumpy before melting
into liquid. Keep stirring, and be careful to not let it burn.

2 Once the sugar has melted and there are no more
clumps, add the butter immediately. Grab a new spoon
and keep stirring until the butter has completely melted, 1 to
2 minutes.

3 Reduce the heat to low and very slowly and carefully
pour in the heavy cream (watch out—it will bubble up
and sputter). Stir continuously for 1 minute, or until the
cream has been incorporated. Remove from the heat and stir
in the salt.

4 Let cool for a few minutes in the pan and then pour into
a glass jar. Store in the refrigerator for up to 2 weeks.
Warm in the microwave for 30 seconds before serving.

MAKES
24
cupcakes

- - - - - -

PREP
25 min

- - - - - -

COOK
18—20 min

- - - - - -

TOTAL
43—45 min

COOKIES 'N' CREAM

cupcakes

Cupcakes really are one of my favorite treats to make, not only because they are cute as can be, but because I may be a tad bit obsessed with frosting. Satisfy your sweet tooth with these rich and tender chocolate cupcakes topped with a cookies 'n' cream frosting. If you must, you can also turn this recipe into a classic chocolate cupcake by omitting the Oreos in the batter and the frosting. But really, why would you?

♥

For the cupcakes

1 cup all-purpose flour

¾ cup unsweetened cocoa powder

1 teaspoon baking soda

1 teaspoon baking powder

1 teaspoon salt

3 large eggs, at room temperature

⅔ cup vegetable oil

¾ cup granulated sugar

¾ cup packed light brown sugar

1 cup sour cream

1 tablespoon vanilla extract

¾ cup milk chocolate or semisweet chocolate chips

24 Oreo cookies (optional)

For the frosting

1 cup (2 sticks) salted butter, at room temperature

3½ to 4 cups powdered sugar

2 teaspoons vanilla extract

5 to 7 teaspoons heavy cream

10 Oreo cookies, crushed into fine crumbs

12 Oreo cookies, cut in half, or 24 mini Oreo cookies (optional)

1 **Make the cupcakes:** Preheat the oven to 350°F. Line two muffin tins with paper liners.

2 In a medium bowl, whisk together the flour, cocoa powder, baking soda, baking powder, and salt.

3 In a large bowl, using a hand mixer, mix together the eggs and oil. Add the granulated sugar, brown sugar, sour cream, and vanilla and mix until combined and the batter is smooth and creamy. Stir in the dry ingredients and mix until just combined. Gently stir in the chocolate chips.

4 Add 1 tablespoon of the batter to the bottom of each muffin cup and then press one Oreo (if using) into each cup. Add 1 to 2 tablespoons more batter, filling the cups two-thirds full. Bake for 18 to 20 minutes, or until a toothpick inserted into the center comes out clean. Let cool in the pan for a few minutes and then transfer to a wire rack to cool completely.

5 **Make the frosting:** While the cupcakes are cooling, in a medium bowl, using a hand mixer, beat the butter until fluffy. Slowly add the powdered sugar and vanilla and mix until smooth and creamy. Add the cream, 1 teaspoon at a time, as needed to thin out the frosting. You want the frosting to be stiff, but still spreadable. Stir in the cookie crumbs. Transfer the frosting to a piping bag fitted with a large round tip (or use a zip-top bag with one corner snipped off) and frost the cupcakes. (Alternatively, you can spread the frosting on with a spatula.)

6 For an extra-special touch, add half an Oreo (or a mini Oreo) to the top of each cupcake.

HELPFUL TIP

If a recipe calls for butter or eggs "at room temperature" and you don't have time to let them sit out before you begin the recipe, try these shortcuts: Place the butter in the microwave at 50% power for 30 to 45 seconds, or until softened. Place the eggs in warm water for a couple of minutes.

BIRTHDAY CUPCAKES

These make a fun gift for someone's special day. I find that homemade gifts are always the best kind to give.

All you need to do for this gift is place a cupcake in a small 9-ounce clear cup and then place the cup in a clear cellophane bag. Tie with ribbon and add a note. Easy, cute, and yummy! Now who wouldn't love a little cupcake surprise on their birthday?

Another way I like to package these is by placing them in a bakery box tied with fabric scraps or ribbon.

i heart crafts

SUNDAE KITS

Want to make someone's day? Surprise them with an
ice cream sundae kit. I love surprises! And I love to see someone's eyes
light up when I hand them a pretty package.

All you need for this kit is to package up the Homemade Hot Fudge (page 249) and
Dreamy Caramel Sauce (page 242) in jars. Then place the jars in a basket with ice cream
sundae cups, spoons, and toppings. You can also attach cute labels or tags to the jars for a
personalized touch. Photocopy a tag from page 254, or download a printable version from
my website at www.iheartnaptime.net/book-template.

My favorite places to find cute baskets are Hobby Lobby, Michael's, and Target.

MAKES
3 CUPS
- - - - - -
PREP
5 min
- - - - - -
COOK
5 min
- - - - - -
TOTAL
10 min

HOMEMADE

hot fudge

This hot fudge sauce is extra rich and smooth, and it is the ultimate topping for any ice cream sundae. It's easy to make with ingredients readily available in your pantry—perfect for a last-minute chocolate craving.

♥

1 In a large saucepan, combine the chocolate chips, sugar, evaporated milk, and butter and heat over medium-low heat, stirring continuously, until the chocolate, sugar, and butter have melted and the mixture comes to a light boil, 5 to 7 minutes. Remove the pan from the heat and stir in the vanilla. Let cool for 5 to 10 minutes before serving; it will thicken as it cools.

2 Store in a glass jar in the refrigerator for up to 2 weeks. Reheat in the microwave, in 30-second intervals, until hot.

2 cups semisweet chocolate chips
¾ cup sugar
1 (12-ounce) can evaporated milk
2 tablespoons salted butter
½ teaspoon vanilla extract

CRAFT

TEMPLATES

To easily re-create the crafts in this
book, copy the following templates from the book,
or download printable versions online at
www.iheartnaptime.net/book-template.

Happy Birthday

Happy Birthday

Happy Birthday

CUT

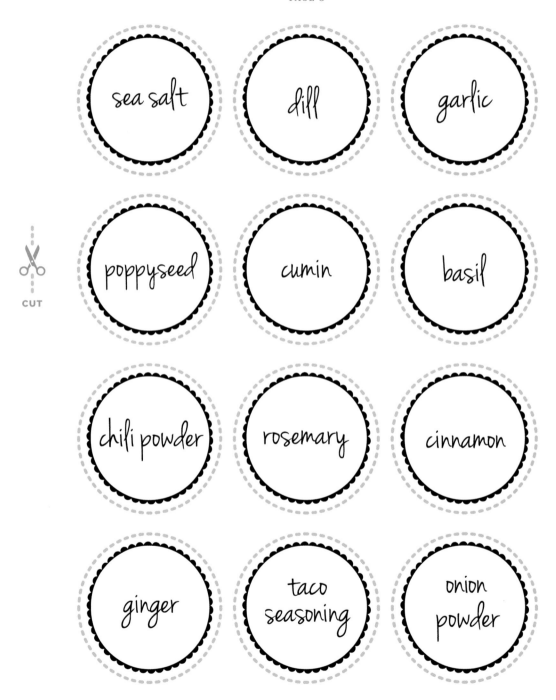

sea salt

dill

garlic

poppyseed

cumin

basil

chili powder

rosemary

cinnamon

ginger

taco seasoning

onion powder

CUT

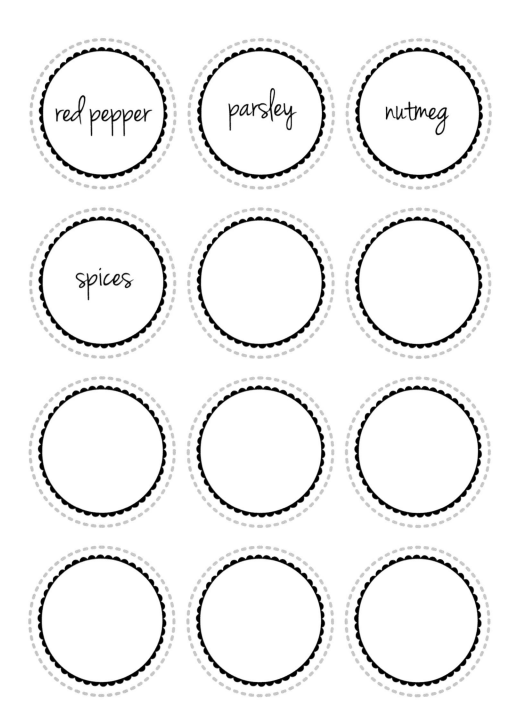

red pepper

parsley

nutmeg

spices

DIY VASE GIFT TAG

PAGE 167

CUT

Thanks a bunch!

SUNDAE KIT GIFT TAGS

PAGE 247

CUT

Caramel

Hot fudge

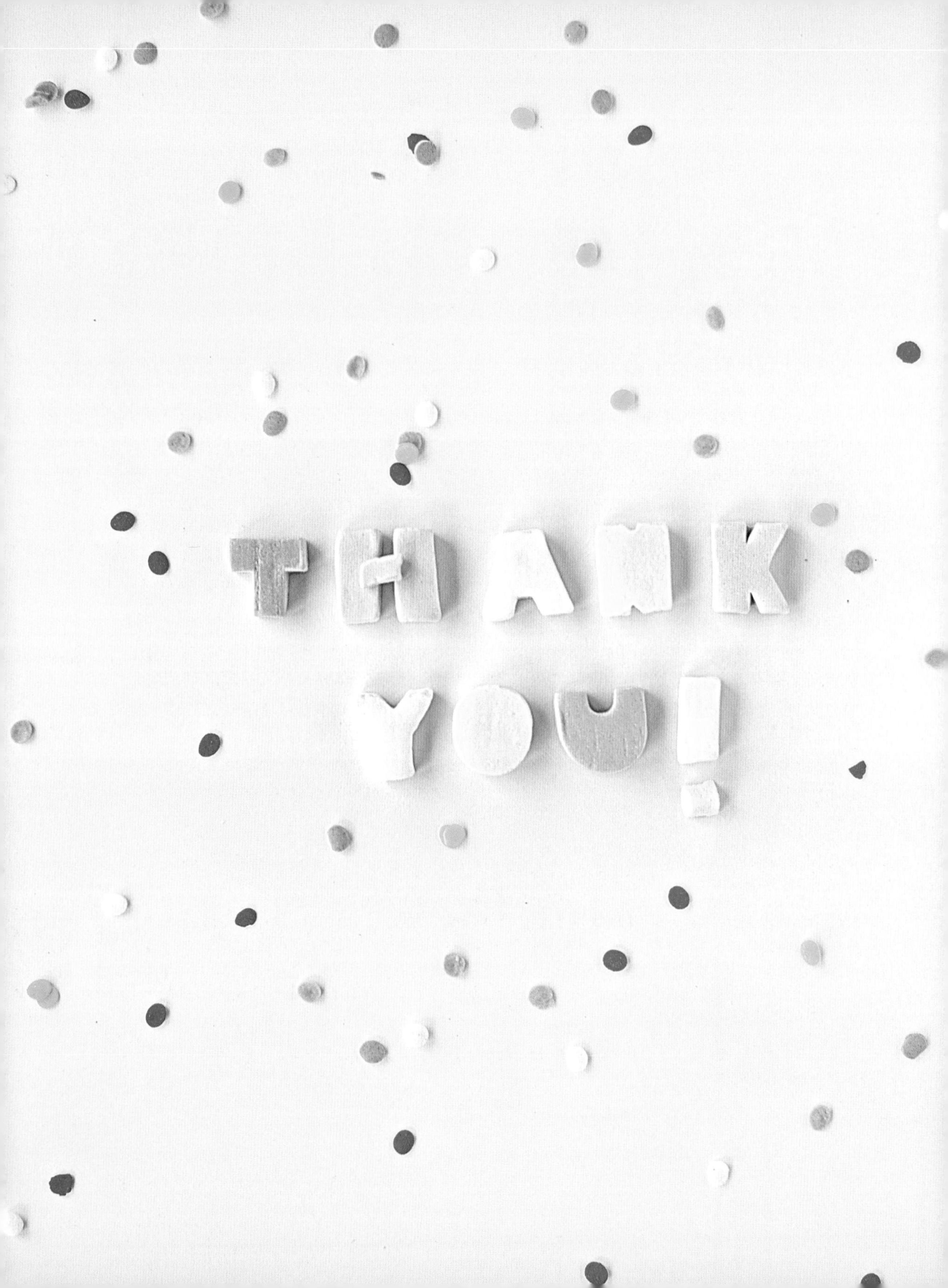
THANK
YOU!

· Acknowledgments ·

Writing a book is one of the hardest and most rewarding things
I have ever done. There is no way this book would have been possible without the help
of these fabulous people. I am so grateful for each and every one of you.

To my best friend and biggest supporter, **DERIC**. This book would not be possible without you. Thanks for making countless trips to the store when I needed last-minute ingredients, eating the same meal night after night (until I got the recipe just right), taking the kids to the park and movies while I worked, listening, and celebrating with me along the way. I certainly lucked out in the husband department. Love you!

To my **BEAUTIFUL CHILDREN**. Carson, thank you for all your wonderful ideas for the book and being such a great helper. Emmalyn, thank you for being such a fabulous assistant in the kitchen. You were both the best taste-testers around. Adalyn, thank you for allowing me to write this book and inspiring most of the recipes inside. To any future children I may have…I cannot wait to bake together! Love you to the moon and back.

Lots of love to my **MOM AND DAD**, for always believing in me, inspiring me to work hard, and encouraging me to reach for my dreams. And a big thanks to my mom for coming to my home for ten days in April to help with dishes, laundry, and edits, and for playing with the kids while I finished the book.

To my **GRAMMA**, thank you for inspiring my love of cooking at such an early age. Thanks for letting me be your kitchen helper and always letting me taste the mashed potatoes and gravy before anyone else.

To **MICHELLE**, thank you for testing recipes, helping behind the scenes, and being the best sister I could ask for.

I would also like to give thanks to **GOD** for giving me inspiration, strength, and courage along the way.

To my **ORTHO WIVES**, I don't know how I would have survived residency without our GNOs and ice cream dates. Thanks for all your love and support.

And to **NATALIE**, thanks for all your help in the kitchen. I couldn't have done it without your help on Mondays!

To all my **WONDERFUL FAMILY AND FRIENDS**, thank you for your constant love, words of encouragement, and support. And thank you for eating leftovers and telling me what was totally great and what was not so great.

To my agent, **STACEY GLICK**, thank you endlessly for all your support and faith in this book. This book wouldn't be here without you!

To my editor, **SARAH PELZ**, and the **ENTIRE TEAM AT GRAND CENTRAL PUBLISHING**. You have been a dream to work with. Thank you for believing in my vision for this book and your enthusiasm and encouragement along the way.

I am so grateful to my head recipe tester, **KATE KNAPP**, who tested every single recipe and made sure they were all perfect. I couldn't have done it without you. And thank you to my ridiculously talented army of recipe testers (all seventy-two of you!)…there are too many people to name, but I sincerely appreciate each one of you for helping make the recipes in this book the best they could be.

To **ANGIE**, from Angela Gerber Photography, for capturing the beautiful photos of my family.

Thank you to everyone on the **I HEART NAPTIME TEAM** who kept my blog running while I was writing this book. I have the best contributors in the world, and the blog would not be the same without your inspiring posts.

To **NAPS**…because where would we be without them?

And to **CHOCOLATE**, because…well, it's chocolate, and it got me through some late nights.

And last, but certainly not least, thanks to you, my **LOVELY READERS**. This book would certainly not be here without you. Thank you for being as obsessed with naptime and dessert as I am. Thank you for your encouraging comments, making my recipes, and purchasing this book. Your support and enthusiasm mean the world to me.

I am forever grateful for all of you. What an amazing journey it's been!

xo-Jamielyn

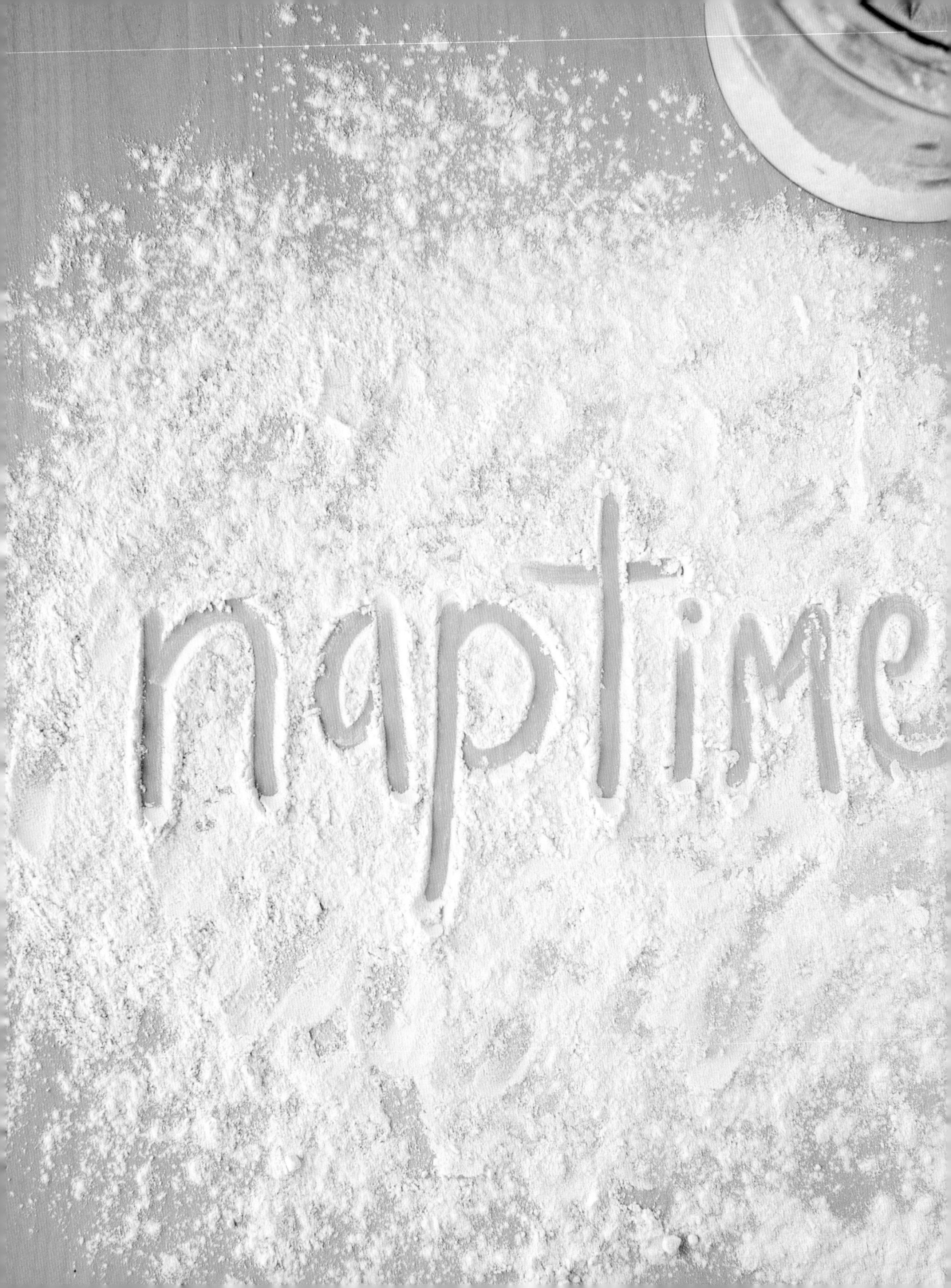
naptime

· Converting to Metrics ·

VOLUME MEASUREMENT CONVERSIONS

Cups	Tablespoons	Teaspoons	Milliliters
		1 tsp	5 ml
1/16 cup	1 tbsp	3 tsp	15 ml
1/8 cup	2 tbsp	6 tsp	30 ml
1/4 cup	4 tbsp	12 tsp	60 ml
1/3 cup	5 1/3 tbsp	16 tsp	80 ml
1/2 cup	8 tbsp	24 tsp	120 ml
2/3 cup	10 2/3 tbsp	32 tsp	160 ml
3/4 cup	12 tbsp	36 tsp	180 ml
1 cup	16 tbsp	48 tsp	240 ml

WEIGHT CONVERSION MEASUREMENTS

US	Metric
1 ounce	28.4 grams (g)
8 ounces	227 g
16 ounces (1 pound)	454 g

COOKING TEMPERATURE CONVERSIONS

Celsius/Centigrade	$F = (C \times 1.8) + 32$
Fahrenheit	$C = (F - 32) \times 0.5556$

Zero degrees Celsius and 100°C are arbitrarily placed at the melting and boiling points of water, while Fahrenheit establishes 0°F as the stabilized temperature when equal amounts of ice, water, and salt are mixed. So, for example, if you are baking at 350°F and want to know that temperature in Celsius, the following calculation will provide it: $C = (350 - 32) \times 0.5556 = 176.68°C$.

· Index ·

· About the Author ·

JAMIELYN NYE is an author, recipe developer, food stylist, and the founder of *I Heart Naptime*, a popular food and lifestyle blog with monthly views in the millions. She aspires to reach women, get their creative juices flowing, and genuinely inspire them.

With a drive to create beauty in her life and delicious food for her darling hubby, and the desire to truly make a difference, she hit the ground running. Her pictures tell stories, and her stories make it simple and easy for her fans to begin creating.

Her unique recipes and craft projects have been featured on many popular websites, including *Better Homes and Garden*, *Martha Stewart*, *People*, *Real Simple*, *Today*, and *Country Living*, among others.

When she's not creating, Jamielyn loves to chase her three little monkeys and snuggle up on the couch with her man. She enjoys dreaming up delicious recipes, thrifting, and thinking of all the possibilities an old treasure can become. Jamielyn loves hunting down the best bakery in each city she visits and enjoys life with her family in Ohio (but don't be mistaken…she is a true Arizona girl at heart).

CONNECT WITH JAMIELYN ON THE WEB: www.iheartnaptime.net

INSTAGRAM	FACEBOOK	TWITTER	PINTEREST
@iheartnaptime	iheartnaptime	@iheartnaptime	iheartnaptime